POWER
AND
PROFITS

POWER
AND
PROFITS

U.S. Policy in
Central America

RONALD W. COX

THE UNIVERSITY PRESS OF KENTUCKY

Copyright © 1994 by The University Press of Kentucky

Scholarly publisher for the Commonwealth,
serving Bellarmine College, Berea College, Centre
College of Kentucky, Eastern Kentucky University,
The Filson Club, Georgetown College, Kentucky
Historical Society, Kentucky State University,
Morehead State University, Murray State University,
Northern Kentucky University, Transylvania University,
University of Kentucky, University of Louisville,
and Western Kentucky University.

Editorial and Sales Offices: Lexington, Kentucky 40508-4008

Library of Congress Cataloging-in-Publication Data

Cox, Ronald W., 1962-
    Power and profits : U.S. policy in Central America / Ronald W. Cox
    p. cm.
    Includes bibliographical references and index.
    ISBN 0-8131-1865-4 (Acid-free)
    1. United States—Foreign economic relations—Central America.
2. Central America—Foreign economic relations—United States.
3. United States—Economic policy.   4. Central America—Economic
policy.   5. Economic interest groupings—United States.
6. Industrial concentration—Central America.   I. Title.
HF1456.5.C4C69   1994
337.730728—dc20   93-41718

This book is dedicated to
my parents and Laura Leigh

Contents

Acknowledgments

The years of research, writing, and preparation of this book would simply not have been possible without the help of associates and the encouragement of close friends. I owe a debt of gratitude to David Gibbs, who encouraged me to apply the "business conflict" model to a historical study of U.S. foreign economic policy toward Central America. The staff of the Eisenhower and Johnson presidential libraries were extremely helpful in locating documents relating to this project. My colleagues at Florida International University took the time to read and comment on my project prior to its completion. The Latin American and Caribbean Center at FIU provided timely funding to undertake additional research at the National Archives and the Library of Congress to complete the project. David Benson was extremely helpful with technical matters that facilitated completion of the manuscript. My friend and colleague Taye Woldesmiate provided me with a valuable example of what it means to be a scholar.

Much thanks goes to Michael Barnett and Rob McCalla of the University of Wisconsin for their helpful comments in the revision of this manuscript. My conversations with Jim Nolt of Vanderbilt University, as well as his valuable research in the area of business-state relations, were useful in adding finishing touches to the project. Tom McCormick and Joel Rogers of the University of Wisconsin also provided helpful advice that guided me in this project.

1
Explaining U.S. Foreign Economic Policy: Toward a Business Conflict Model

This study examines the relationship between business groups and the state in the formulation of U.S. foreign economic policy. Within the last twenty years, scholars from various perspectives have modified and refined their theoretical frameworks regarding the relationship between business and the state. Qualifying their earlier approaches, some pluralists have developed models of U.S. foreign economic policy that emphasize the political advantages derived by business groups that are economically powerful.[1] Others have cautioned against the notion that economic power can be translated so easily into political influence.[2]

From a different perspective, marxists have rejected the proposition that the state is a captive of the capitalist class. Instead, many have insisted that the state is capable of acting against the interests of powerful business groups when it comes to particular issues or socioeconomic circumstances.[3] Statist theorists, meanwhile, argue that pluralists and marxists are both incorrect. They insist that the state acts in the "national interest," which overrides the interests of capitalists or the narrow agendas of other powerful interest groups.

For the purposes of brevity and precision, these various approaches to foreign economic policy can be divided into two broad categories. First, there are state-centered approaches, which emphasize the institutional structures of the state and the autonomy of political and administrative officials within the state (an orientation that includes realist and marxist variants).[4] Second, there are society-centered approaches, which view U.S. policy as a reflection of competition among interest groups or political parties (pluralist approach) or as a

product of the interests of dominant classes or groups in society (marxist and elitist approaches).[5] This study borrows from society-centered
approaches to construct a plausible explanation of U.S. foreign economic policy toward Central America in the post-World War II period.

Drawing upon insights from a number of scholarly sources, including David Gibbs, Jeffrey Frieden, and Thomas Ferguson, I will
construct a business conflict model of U.S. policy that challenges the
propositions of the state-centered approaches.[6] Briefly stated, the argument is that business groups have played a dominant role in pressuring government officials to adopt foreign investment, trade, and
aid strategies toward Central America. In addition, divisions among
competing business groups have affected governmental debates over
foreign economic policy.

The task of this chapter is threefold. First, I will compare and
contrast state-centered and society-centered approaches to U.S. foreign economic policy in order to locate the business conflict model
within the parameters of competing perspectives. Second, I will elu-
cidate and develop the business conflict model theoretically, to dem-
onstrate its relevance to the subject matter. Finally, I will provide an
overview of how this study uses the model, with a discussion of the
methodology of the study and a summary of the application of the
model to the various stages of U.S. policy toward Central America.

State-centered Approaches

In many studies of the formulation of U.S. foreign economic policy,
business is thought to be a player secondary to the broader national
security goals of the United States. Proponents of this view argue
that the U.S. state formulates policy as a rational actor, with a predominant national interest in maintaining its security against the
ever-present threat of encroachment by other states in an anarchic
world. In this approach, the state has a national interest that overrides the particularistic concerns of any one societal group.[7]

From time to time the state seeks the cooperation and support of
business groups in the implementation of foreign policy programs,
but ultimately the state establishes the policy-making boundaries that
guide the participation of business. The degree to which business
participates in foreign policy making is determined by decisions made
by state actors independent of business pressures. In this model, state
actors are most influenced by their assessment of the "national inter-

est," which is always conditioned by the anarchic environment of the international political system.

State-centered theorists argue that U.S. foreign economic policy has been based on national security concerns, specifically the threat of communism. Thus one would expect U.S. policy makers to formulate foreign economic policy as part of a broader effort to counter perceived threats to geostrategic interests. In applications of state-centered theory to U.S. foreign economic policy toward Central America, institutional actors are said to be motivated by anticommunism and not by pressure from business interests.[8]

The claim here is not that statist theorists are unable to formulate useful insights regarding foreign economic policy. Instead, the argument advanced is that state-centered theory by itself is incapable of explaining the *content* of specific foreign economic policies that the U.S. adopted toward Central America. Makers of foreign policy may pursue a wide variety of policy measures designed to counter communist aggression or threats to national security. However, the ideology of anticommunism is often unable to explain why policy makers chose a particular foreign economic policy over alternatives, especially when all of the policy options could have been justified on national security grounds.

Society-centered Approaches

Numerous scholars challenge the statist claim that the state is a "rational actor" with "national interests."[9] Their approach differs from the statist model in several ways. First, there is an emphasis on the relationship between domestic interest groups and the state in the formulation of foreign economic policy. Domestic groups advance their foreign policy goals by pressuring the state to formulate and implement policies favored by particular interests. As noted earlier, there are both pluralist and marxist versions of such efforts. Second, there is an attempt to relate the international interests of domestic groups to the formulation of foreign economic policies.[10]

Society-centered theorists criticize statists for exaggerating the extent to which the state is autonomous in relation to societal actors. This is especially the case in the area of foreign economic policy, where business groups stand to gain or lose from the adoption of particular policies. Business groups affected directly by U.S. legislation regarding foreign investment, trade, and aid policies have an incentive to organize. Because of their economic interests, policy expertise, and political connections, they often can avoid the collective action problems facing the general public on questions of foreign economic policy.[11]

This study uses insights from several diverse theorists who emphasize society-centered variables in their discussion of foreign economic policy. Pluralists, marxists, and some bureaucratic theorists have emphasized the importance of pressure groups in the formulation of policy.[12] These theorists have made important contributions by directing our attention to macroeconomic and organizational factors that condition interest group pressure. This study builds on a tradition of society-centered approaches to U.S. foreign economic policy.

However, this study differs in important ways from other society-centered approaches. First, the business conflict model differs from pluralist accounts by emphasizing the dominant role of business groups in the formulation and implementation of policy. Most pluralists now accept the fact that business is not just another interest group.[13] At the same time, pluralists still contend that business is one player among many with an opportunity to influence policy, and that business influence is conditioned by the relative strength of other organized groups. This study will argue that, in the case of Central America, business groups have often been able to shape and direct U.S. foreign investment and trade strategy independent of other pressure groups.

This study shares with marxist accounts a focus on class-based determinants of U.S. foreign economic policy. As in other marxist accounts, business firms are viewed as being motivated by profit maximization in their pursuit of foreign investment and trade strategies. Business groups with direct investments in Central America (internationalists) have pressured U.S. policy makers to devise market schemes that would maximize profit-making opportunities and reduce costs. Other business groups tied to the U.S. market (nationalists) have often clashed with internationalists over the form and content of U.S. trade, aid, and investment policies in the region.

This study differs from some marxist accounts in its attention to the structural constraints that limit the ability of business groups and corporations to attain their preferred foreign economic policies. Business groups are forced to react to changes in the international environment, which condition the nature of business pressure on policy makers. In addition, business groups must articulate their interests to foreign policy makers within a particular institutional setting that establishes the boundaries for pressure group strategies. The next section discusses the nature of business conflict and the various structural constraints that condition business influence on foreign economic policy.

An Overview of the Business Conflict Model

Critics of the business conflict model will surely ask why business is identified as the dominant influence in U.S. foreign economic policy. What about national security considerations, the relative influence of competing interest groups, and the self-interest of bureaucracies in the formulation of foreign economic policy? The business conflict model does not discount the importance of these other variables. Instead, the model argues that policy making cannot be understood in terms of these variables alone.

The ability of business groups to influence policy is conditioned by a number of factors that will be examined in subsequent sections. First, business groups must be able to overcome the collective action problems inherent in building organizations that can effectively influence policy. Second, business influence is mediated and structured by sectoral competition with other business groups and by the opportunities and obstacles posed by political institutions, national security considerations, and class conflict or instability in the less-developed world.

In the area of foreign trade and investment policies, business groups possess several advantages over rival interest groups in overcoming collective action problems.[14] First, business groups control economic and intellectual resources that policy makers rely on to implement foreign economic policies. As a result, high-level foreign policy officials in the Departments of State, Commerce, Defense and Treasury often solicit business support economically and politically prior to the formulation of policy and during the its implementation. Business groups are given opportunities to influence policy at the highest levels of the foreign policy executive, including the White House and State, Defense, Treasury, and Commerce, which are often denied to other interest groups.

This access to the foreign policy executive is dominated by business internationalists or firms characterized by relatively high levels of foreign direct investment and trade.[15] Internationally oriented firms have established links to the executive branch as a result of their particular economic status and political organization. Unlike other domestic interest groups, internationalist firms have a vested interest in a wide range of foreign economic policies that affect their foreign investments. These firms are also well-positioned to work with the executive branch on short- and long-term foreign economic policies toward the less-developed world.

There are several reasons why business internationalists enjoy a close working relationship with the foreign policy executive. First, government officials are often business executives themselves, on leaves of absence or between jobs with law firms or major corporations. Of the foreign policy elite concentrated in the upper strata of the most important bureaucracies—the secretaries, under secretaries, and assistant secretaries of state, defense, and the treasury and the administrators of the CIA, the National Security Council, Economic Cooperation Administration, the Agency for International Development, and the President's national security adviser—about two-thirds have come from corporate management or law backgrounds since the end of World War II.[16]

Firms engaged in foreign investment and trade tend to dominate the affiliations of the foreign policy elite. As a result, this political elite is often more disposed to listen to a member of the corporate establishment than to interest groups lacking similar connections. As one business executive explained when asked why he had relatively easy access to Foreign policy makers, "The Hill is much more receptive—let's face it—to the establishment, because they are part of the establishment themselves."[17]

The background of policy makers, however, proves little by itself. What is more significant is that business internationalists have built organizations designed to influence and collaborate with foreign policy officials on questions of foreign trade and investment. Direct foreign investors are represented by an umbrella of internationalist organizations, which are discussed throughout this study. The organizations include the Committee for Economic Development, the Council on Foreign Relations, the National Planning Association, the Business Advisory Council, and the International Chambers of Commerce.[18] These organizations have produced position papers and private advisory bodies that have worked with the executive branch in devising foreign economic strategies toward the less-developed world.

Toward Latin America specifically, the Business Group for Latin America and later the Council of the Americas and Caribbean/Central American Action, as well as the Association of American Chambers of Commerce in Latin America, have been important organizations for internationalists influential in foreign economic policy. Today the Council of the Americas is the largest and single most influential private organization to lobby for corporate interests. The council represents a continuation of corporate organizations that have contributed to the formulation of U.S. foreign economic policy toward the region and elsewhere in the world.

In a study of the council's lobbying efforts on Capitol Hill, Lars Schoultz summarizes the membership and organizational strengths of the organization:

The Council of the Americas is a nonprofit business association supported by over two hundred member corporations with investments in Latin America. It is the nation's most influential nongovernmental organization with a specific interest in Latin America. Its corporate members represent 90 percent of U.S. equity in Latin America and include virtually every major multinational corporation based in the United States. The Council's major strength lies in its ability to link executives of member corporations and foreign policy makers at the highest levels of government. . . . In the area of U.S.-Latin American relations, the opinion of a COA [Council of the Americas] affiliated executive is often the only nongovernmental view a major policy maker will hear.[19]

This study focuses on the historical pattern and contemporary structure of international business organizations and their relationship to the foreign policy executive in the formulation and implementation of foreign economic policy toward Central America. I examine not only organizations founded by multinational firms, such as those listed above, but also organizations founded by domestic business groups with little or no export trade and foreign investment. These business nationalists, as a result of their sectoral position in the U.S. economy, generally favor a different set of foreign trade and investment policies than do their internationalist counterparts.

Business nationalists are represented historically by local Chambers of Commerce and various trade associations.[20] These organizations have not enjoyed the extensive connections to the foreign policy executive that have characterized business internationalists. As a result, they have had to employ the most visible forms of lobbying, such as testifying before congressional committees and subcommittees, public appeals, letter writing, and the like.[21]

The business conflict model posits that internationalists and nationalists have been divided by sectoral economic interests in their demands for foreign economic policies and that such divisions have been reflected in policy outcomes. In addition, internationalists have

themselves been divided over foreign economic strategies. The next
section examines the theoretical importance of such divisions in understanding the business conflict model.

Business Groups and Sectoral Conflict

Business groups have different policy preferences as a result of their
sectoral location within the international and domestic economies.
One of the most important sectoral distinctions is that between firms
that engage in direct investment abroad and firms tied to the U.S.
market. Borrowing from Helen Milner, "The more sizable and the
more integrated a firm's direct foreign investments are, the more likely it is to resist protection and to prefer open markets."[22] On the
other hand, domestic firms with a relatively minor stake in foreign
investments are more likely to call for protection of the domestic
market.

In addition, firms exhibiting greater export dependence are more
likely to favor efforts to liberalize trade than firms with low export
dependence. This is true for three reasons. First, the "closing of a
home market may prompt retaliation by foreign governments."[23]
Such retaliation may be especially harmful to export industries dependent on foreign markets. Second, protection of the domestic market is likely to increase costs for export-dependent firms. These costs
may include a reduction of available supplies, which tends to drive
up the price of a firm's product and make it less competitive in foreign markets. Finally, closure of the domestic market may make it
difficult for foreign governments and individuals to earn the foreign
exchange necessary to buy imports, further reducing the foreign
sales of an export-dependent firm.[24]

In the case of Central America, U.S. firms characterized by their
export dependence and foreign direct investments have tended to
advocate liberalization of trade with the region. These internationalists have been opposed by domestic-oriented firms seeking to curb
foreign competition. As I will document during the following chapters, internationalists during the 1950s attempted to pressure the
State Department to liberalize foreign trade with the less-developed
world, only to be frustrated by business nationalists committed to
protectionist policies.

As a result of their inability to lower tariffs significantly in the
U.S. market, internationalists with direct foreign investments in Cen-

tral America began to pressure policy makers to support a Central American Common Market (CACM). The CACM established tariff barriers that allowed for import-substituting industrialization within the region. The CACM proved to be a second-best scenario for U.S. multinational firms able to increase (or to begin) direct foreign investments in Central America. The creation of the CACM allowed U.S. manufacturing firms to expand dramatically their investments and sales in Central America, behind high tariff walls.[25]

In addition, internationalists have worked with executive branch officials to devise and implement aid programs for the CACM. In the late 1950s and early 1960s, business groups lobbied for aid to strengthen the CACM. U.S. aid programs provided for the infrastructural needs of U.S. firms seeking to expand or begin their investments in the region. Aid programs also offered a series of investment incentives, including tax breaks and subsidies, for U.S. manufacturing firms investing behind the tariff walls of the CACM.

The "solution" of the CACM did not satisfy all internationalists, however. Those firms characterized by both high export dependence and low foreign direct investments were sometimes unable to take advantage of the CACM. Instead, export-dependent firms were hurt by the high tariff walls surrounding the common market, since it interfered with their ability to export to the region. These firms emerged as early critics of the CACM and its protectionist policies.

As the Central American Common Market broke down because of a series of economic and political problems, many U.S. firms in the 1970s began to shift from import-substitution industrialization to export promotion. Here, as we will see in the final chapters of this study, there emerged new tensions between U.S. firms, based largely on the different types of sectoral investments in the region. Put simply, firms characterized by labor-intensive investments (metal products, textiles, machinery, chemicals, foodstuffs, and accessory construction) favored a different set of U.S. foreign economic policies than firms that were not labor-intensive (commercial banking, petroleum, food and beverage processing).[26]

Labor-intensive firms form the core of what James Kurth has called an interventionist coalition in U.S. foreign policy toward the region.[27] Faced with tight wage restraints, these firms have supported U.S. military assistance to governments faced with leftist insurgencies and/or militant labor movements. Organized within the Association of Chambers of Commerce in Latin America, these agribusiness, textile, and other manufacturing firms have aggressively supported U.S. military aid to, and at times military intervention in, Guatemala, El Salvador, and Nicaragua. These firms depend on brutal military dictatorships to police and control the labor force in Central America, since the low labor costs are especially important to the international competitiveness of these firms.

Other interests in the U.S. that favored a militarization of U.S. policy toward Central America in the 1970s and 1980s included corporations tied to the military-industrial complex. Defense contractors joined with right-wing intellectuals and former executive branch officials to form the Committee on the Present Danger. The committee began advocating increased military aid to Central American governments in the mid-1970s. They were frustrated with the slow response of the Carter administration, which continued to pursue a human rights policy, although unevenly, toward the region. By the 1980s, various members of the committee had secured positions within the Reagan administration's foreign policy bureaucracy, where they began to influence policy formulation.[28]

Firms that are less labor-intensive and that have no ties to the military-industrial complex tend to advocate economic, as opposed to military, assistance to the region. These firms also are willing to support a wider variety of regimes than their labor-intensive counterparts. For example, commercial bankers with loans to the Nicaraguan government generally opposed the U.S. policy of arming the contras. Bankers found that they could work with the Sandinista regime as long as it promised to repay its international loans. They argued that the Reagan administration's policies were creating political instability that interfered with international financial transactions and blocked a profitable climate for foreign investment.[29]

In this study, I will document the battles among business groups with diverse sectoral interests in an effort to illustrate the importance of this aspect of the business conflict model. As we will see in the remainder of this section, business influence is also conditioned by other factors, including the nature of political institutions, national security considerations, and the level of class conflict and/or instability in the less-developed world.

The Institutions: Executive Branch and Congress

Business interests seeking to influence U.S. foreign economic policy must communicate their policy preferences to political elites within the executive and legislative branches. The institutional structures of the U.S. state therefore constrain and condition the nature of business group pressure. In particular, interbranch rivalries between the executive and Congress affect the relative influence of business internationalists and nationalists in foreign economic policy.

The business conflict model posits three propositions regarding the effect of institutional arrangements on business conflict. First, business internationalists have more opportunities than business nationalists to influence the executive branch in the formulation of foreign economic policies. This means that institutional reforms strengthening the authority of the executive branch will generally result in greater influence for business internationalists.

The most important reform of executive-legislative relations was the passage of the Reciprocal Trade Agreements Act of 1934. Although the act had little immediate impact, given the economic conditions of the 1930s, the long-term result was to strengthen the hand of the executive branch by shifting tariff-making authority from Congress to the executive.[30] As a result, business internationalists close to the executive branch gained influence in foreign economic policy making relative to their nationalist counterparts.

The second proposition is that business nationalists and internationalists compete for influence over Congress in foreign economic policy. Business nationalists lack the wealth, policy expertise, and political connections of their internationalist counterparts. As a result, they devote most of their political efforts to lobbying key congressional committees that influence foreign economic policy. The disparate and diffuse membership of Congress allows business nationalists to gain influence through firm-centered lobbying strategies directed toward individual Congressmen.

In the area of foreign economic policy, business nationalist groups and firms often target key congressional committees such as the House Ways and Means Committee and the Senate Finance Committee. Nationalist firms are especially influential with the Senate Finance Committee, which has "a reputation of being more protectionist, more receptive to special interests, and less cooperative with the Executive than its legislative counterpart [the House Ways and Means Committee]."[31] As one scholar put it, "The dispersion of power makes the Senate less resistant to a logrolling process, and this tendency is reinforced by the flexibility of the rules which govern its operations."[32]

Business nationalists are able to take advantage of the dispersal of authority within Congress to articulate sectoral demands in the area of trade and aid policies. Nationalists are able to exercise relatively more influence upon policy formulation when the policy process encourages special amendments, as it does in the Senate. There the chairperson of the Senate Finance Committee faces unlimited debate over a bill unless cloture is called, a possibility that encourages an unlimited number of special amendments.[33]

In addition, recent scholarly studies have shown that the increasing number of subcommittees within the House after 1973 has tended to increase the relative influence of protectionist groups.[34] The reason is that committee chairpersons are often less able to centralize control over staff and information than was previously the case. The loss of power by the chairperson of the House Ways and Means Committee has given greater opportunities to special interests promoting restrictive trade practices.

The third proposition is that interbranch conflict over trade and aid both reflects and impacts upon business conflict between internationalists and nationalists. Internationalists use their connections with the executive branch to promote liberal trade and aid policies. Nationalists use their congressional connections to implement trade restrictions and to limit foreign aid. The results of interbranch rivalries are often compromises over trade and aid proposals.

However there are important qualifiers to these broad propositions. At times internationalists devote considerable energy to lobbying Congress, tending to be more effective in cases when congressional decision making is relatively centralized in the hands of a strong committee chairman sympathetic to liberal trade and aid policies. Nationalists tend to prevail in cases where congressional authority is dispersed *and* when the executive branch is weakened in its ability to influence policy.

At times nationalists are also able to take advantage of bureaucratic conflict within the executive branch to gain influence in foreign economic policy. Divisions between executive branch officials along nationalist-internationalist lines influence and condition business conflict over foreign economic policy. Sometimes such divisions are a reflection of business connections to executive branch policy makers. At other times, bureaucratic competition and compromise are driven by the ideologies of individual policy makers.[35]

The degree to which the executive branch can successfully promote liberal trade and aid policies is constrained by other factors that structure business conflict over foreign economic policy. These include national security considerations, which impact upon inter-branch conflict and policy outcomes.

The Question of National Security

Most studies of U.S. foreign policy counterpose national security interests with business interests. The conventional logic assumes that business will have minimal influence on policy in cases where national security interests dominate. This study argues that the conventional view is wrong regarding U.S. foreign economic policy toward Central America. The business conflict model argues that the influence of business internationalists on U.S. policy was often greater during times of "tight bipolarity," or heightened global competition between the United States the former Soviet Union.

Two propositions are advanced regarding the relationship between business influence and national security policy. First, under conditions of tight bipolarity in the international arena, the executive branch has increased autonomy from Congress in the formulation and implementation of foreign economic policy toward the less-developed world. Specifically, the White House, the State Department, and the National Security Council have a greater ability to circumvent Congress in foreign policy making during times of heightened global competition. In the case of Central America, the cold war of the late 1950s and early 1960s and the second cold war of the late 1970s and early 1980s helped give impetus to dramatic increases in aid programs designed and administered by the executive branch.

The second proposition is that business internationalists with close ties to the executive branch gain increased influence over U.S. foreign economic policy during times of tight bipolarity. At the same time, business nationalists and firms exclusively dependent on congressional lobbying lose influence relative to their internationalist counterparts. In the late 1950s and early 1960s, business internationalists worked formally and informally with members of the executive branch to devise foreign economic programs designed simultaneously to counter "national security threats" to U.S. interests and to bolster the position of U.S. foreign investors in the region.

Business internationalists, unlike their nationalist counterparts, are positioned at the crossroads of U.S. foreign economic policy, with economic interests both at home and abroad. In this regard, their interests often coincide with the national security objectives of the foreign policy executive. Thus business officials and foreign policy bureaucrats have a close working relationship that is documented in this study, including a propensity to establish organizational links designed to formulate short- and long-term foreign economic policies toward Central America. In the case of the first cold war, the Business Group for Latin America was a key player in facilitating this linkage. By the second cold war, business firms within the Association of American Chambers of Commerce in Latin America and the business group Caribbean/Central American Action were vying for influence within the executive branch under both Carter and Reagan.

This study will argue that national security considerations cannot be separated from business influence in any neat fashion. Instead, business conflict is conditioned, affected, and mediated by such considerations in the making of foreign economic policy. However, the business conflict model, as opposed to statist theory, is often better able to explain the content of foreign economic policies. That is, statists cannot use national security considerations alone to explain why some business groups won and others lost in the formulation and implementation of policy.

The range of national security considerations have included both U.S.-Soviet competition and the rise of radical nationalist or communist movements in the less-developed world. Both business internationalists and State Department executives have an interest in formulating policies designed to control and subdue leftist insurgents. Business conflict is often affected and mediated by the level of class conflict and instability in the less-developed world.

Class Conflict and Instability

The business conflict model argues that both business internationalists and policy makers are influenced by the rise of leftist insurgencies and Communist-inspired movements in the less-developed world. As a result of their sectoral interests, however, internationalist business groups and firms advocate different solutions for quelling insurgencies or controlling radical nationalist governments. The business conflict model advances three propositions regarding the relationship between business influence and class conflict.

First, the rise of leftist insurgencies in the less-developed world shifts policymaking authority away from Congress to the executive branch, giving business internationalists more potential influence on policy formulation. The primary objectives of the U.S. government are to control and subdue the leftist insurgency to protect the investment climate for all U.S. corporations. The U.S. government tolerates democratic elections only if there are no mass organizations and movements capable of challenging the economic prerogatives of U.S. investors or if elections are structured to isolate ideological opponents of U.S. policy.[36] Otherwise, the preferred solution is military force backed up by U.S. advisers and U.S. military assistance.

Second, business groups are usually split on the wisdom of using military force to quell insurgency. Those internationalist firms that are labor-intensive usually endorse and support increased military aid to quell the insurgents. Labor-intensive firms often depend on military governments to police the domestic workforce and keep wages low. This is especially important to firms facing strong international competition, which puts a premium on low labor costs.

On the other hand, more competitive firms that are less labor-intensive are less likely to support a military solution to defeat insurgents. These firms are often able to grant concessions to labor and to work with diverse ideological governments in the less developed world. Commercial bankers, for example, have on more than one occasion expressed support for communist regimes as good investment risks for financial capital.[37]

This flexibility when dealing with Third World governments distinguishes such internationalists from their labor-intensive counterparts. Often dubbed "liberal internationalists," these firms advocate economic concessions and bargaining to weaken leftist insurgents. They see an exclusive emphasis on military conflict as undesirable, given the instability it generates and the other possible options for curbing unrest.

The third proposition is that executive branch policies to curb leftist insurgencies are influenced by the relative influence of competing business internationalists. Under the Carter and Reagan administrations, there emerged by 1979 a battle between labor-intensive business firms and liberal internationalists over foreign economic policy. Labor-intensive firms supported increased military aid as a response to the leftist insurgency within El Salvador and the triumph of the Sandinistas in Nicaragua. Liberal internationalists, coauthors of the Miami Report, advocated economic measures and negotiations to challenge leftists in the region. Both groups were able to influence policy in various ways, depending on their political ties to executive branch officials in each administration.

Methodology

This study will test the propositions of the business conflict model by undertaking a historical analysis of U.S. foreign economic policy toward Central America, using U.S. policy toward various Central American countries, especially El Salvador, Guatemala, and Nicaragua, as case studies. The book will trace the relationship between business organizations and the U.S. government during the formulation and implementation of Central American policy in the post-World War II period.

Case studies from Central America are useful for three reasons. First, the United States has intervened extensively in the region since the early 1950s. The United States intervened in 1954 to overthrow the democratically elected government of Arbenz in Guatemala and bolstered the subsequent dictatorship with extensive foreign aid. U.S. foreign policymakers participated in negotiating the terms of the Central American Common Market, which had an important impact on both regional trade and the investment patterns of U.S. corporations. In the late 1970s and early 1980s, U.S. military and economic aid to the region increased dramatically in response to the Nicaraguan revolution and the growth of a rebel movement in El Salvador. In each of these periods, the State Department shifted its foreign economic policies in response to changing domestic and international political and economic factors.

Second, U.S. investment in Central America has been quite low historically compared with investment in the rest of Latin America, especially Mexico, Brazil, and Venezuela. One would not expect business interests to exercise influence on U.S. policy toward a region that represents less than 10 percent of U.S. investment in Latin America. If business interests did in fact determine U.S. foreign economic policy toward countries such as Guatemala, El Salvador, and Nicaragua, then these case studies would provide strong support for the business conflict model.

Third, there are considerable advantages in examining more than one country in the region. As private documents make clear, leading U.S. corporations and government officials often viewed individual

Central American states as part of one larger region. This was especially true after the late 1950s, when business internationalists pushed for a Central American Common Market to facilitate regional investment. It was still true in the late 1970s and early 1980s, when internationalists in the corporate and political establishment viewed political instability in one country as a threat to U.S. economic and political interests in the region as a whole.

In fact, as I will show in chapters 5 and 6, U.S. business groups by the late 1970s often relied on locations throughout the Caribbean Basin (Central America and the Caribbean nations) for international production strategies geared toward the North American market. These companies, especially U.S. manufacturers, increasingly viewed the Caribbean Basin as a vital region for enhancing their international competitiveness through lower production costs and proximity to the advanced North American market. At the same time, U.S. policy makers recognized threats to U.S. security and economic interests in one country as threats to their interests in the entire area.

In addition, multiple case studies allow for a comparative analysis of the different sectoral interests of various business groups in the region. As we will see, business groups often differed over the methods used by the U.S. government in promoting economic and political stability in Central America. These differences hinged on the type of sectoral investments undertaken by U.S. corporations.

For example, commercial bankers were more insulated from regime changes than corporations with direct investments in the region. The fact that commercial banks relied on loans for the bulk of their profits meant that they could often tolerate a more diverse ideological clientele than their manufacturing counterparts, which often relied on the economic and political advantages provided by particular Central American regimes to protect their profit margins. As we will see, these differences were especially apparent in U.S. policy toward Nicaragua in the late 1970s and early 1980s.

The analysis of several countries allows us to develop hypotheses about which business groups exerted more influence on U.S. policy at various conjunctures. For example, while bank loans dominated U.S. investments in Nicaragua, U.S. manufacturing firms were more important in El Salvador. A comparative analysis allows us to see whether these differences had any effect on policy toward individual countries in the region.

The issue of causality is a difficult one for this kind of study. As David Gibbs noted in his study of U.S. intervention in the Congo, powerful business interests do not advertise their connections to foreign policy makers.[38] The statements of public officials do little to establish a connection between business elites and U.S. government actors. Most of the important documents remain classified well after a foreign policy decision is made. Efforts to interview foreign policy makers and business elites often fail to reveal the extent of business influence on particular policies. Even after securing declassified documents illustrating the connections between business interests and foreign policy makers, there is some difficulty in determining causality for any given set of policies. Business influence may be one of several factors determining foreign economic policy, a complication in trying to cite a primary cause for U.S. policy.

None of these problems can be completely overcome in a study that seeks to be both historical and contemporary in focus. However, certain approaches can succeed in minimizing the most serious obstacles to the question of business influence on U.S. foreign policy. First, a sustained and historical case study of one region allows for empirical depth that is essential for this topic. Many of the important documents establishing U.S. policy toward Central America in the 1950s and early 1960s have only recently been declassified. An examination of these documents can help reveal the significance of economic considerations in U.S. foreign policy making.

Second, important business groups have established organizations devoted explicitly to influencing government policy toward Latin America as a whole and Central America specifically. Archival collections at the Council on Foreign Relations library, the presidential libraries, and the National Archives provide some indication of correspondence between business and governmental elites. In addition, publications by the Council on Foreign Relations, the Council of the Americas, and various corporate foundations can give some idea of the position of significant sectors of business on questions of U.S. foreign policy.

This study will rely extensively on primary sources in tracing the development of U.S. policy toward Central America. Declassified documents will be especially important for the early part of this study, including collections at the National Archives and various presidential libraries. Business publications will be used to examine the views of business elites concerning U.S. policy toward El Salvador, Guatemala, and Nicaragua. The role of business organizations in formulating and implementing foreign economic policy will be examined with reference to governmental bodies comprised of both business elites and public officials, such as the Rockefeller Foundation and the Grace Commission. Also, secondary sources such as books and periodicals will be used.

Still, there remains the difficulty of demonstrating influence in foreign economic policy, a topic that has been discussed by a number of scholars, including Joanne Gowa and Bruce Russett in recent works.[39] These theorists correctly note the numerous problems in trying to isolate the influence of a single societal group on U.S. foreign policy making. There is no way to overcome completely the problem of overdetermination in a historical case study. There are so many complexities and ambiguities in the foreign policy process that many influences are likely to be found in any explanation of any particular policy shift.

However, the problem of influence can be managed by insisting on the hardest conditions for a demonstration of influence: 1) that business communicated its aims to policymakers, 2) that policymakers considered business demands, and 3) that policymakers acted upon those demands in the formulation and implementation of foreign economic policy. Even though this demonstration does not prove influence, it does help establish solid criteria for managing the plethora of information to be found in archival material and other primary sources.

At the very least, this study is intended to fill a scholarly gap that exists in regard to the relationship between business and the state in U.S. foreign economic policy. In part because of the methodological problems involved and in part because of ingrained assumptions that dominate the field of international relations, scholars have rarely examined the views of business groups, let alone their relationship to policy makers. This work attempts to fill that void by tracing the evolution of business views on U.S. foreign economic policy toward Central America and the relationship and correspondence between business elites and foreign policy officials.

2

The "Trade Not Aid" Strategy for Third World Industrialization

This chapter examines the role of business groups and U.S. policy makers in developing foreign economic policies for Latin America and the less-developed world during the 1940s and the 1950s. Business internationalists prominent within the Council on Foreign Relations, the National Planning Association, the Committee for Economic Development, and the National Foreign Trade Council drafted proposals during World War II that emphasized the importance of Third World industrialization for U.S. manufacturers. These business groups worked with government planning commissions in the 1940s and the 1950s to devise lending programs to promote the infrastructure necessary for industrial development of Latin America.

Business internationalists in the 1940s and early 1950s hoped to increase the level of direct U.S. investment in less-developed countries with a combination of private sector initiative and minimal bilateral and multilateral aid through Point Four, the Export-Import Bank (EXIM), and the World Bank. They were especially concerned that aid programs be limited so as to complement, not compete with, direct foreign investment. Working with government policy makers, they helped devise the outlines of a "trade, not aid" strategy designed to promote direct foreign investment in manufacturing in less-developed countries. This chapter details the efforts of business groups and government officials to develop the "trade not aid" strategy, with case studies of the Point Four program in El Salvador and U.S. aid for the Inter-American Highway.

In addition, I document the efforts of business internationalists to liberalize U.S. trade barriers that inhibited the promotion of export-led industrialization in the Third World. Internationalists clashed with nationalist business groups over increases in foreign aid and the liberalization of trade. As a result, foreign economic policy during the late 1940s and 1950s often reflected a series of compromises between business factions over the level of government appropriations for the World Bank, EXIM, Point Four, and other efforts to liberalize trade.

As early as World War II, business internationalists expressed their preferences for foreign economic policies that would promote Third World industrialization. The Council on Foreign Relations (CFR) worked closely with government agencies to devise postwar economic strategies designed to facilitate and maintain economic recovery after World War II. An early concern of council members was the possibility of a lack of sufficient demand for manufactured goods produced by U.S. companies.

A related concern was that the United States would suffer from structural imbalances in the domestic economy as a result of "the over-development of heavy industry during World War II."[1] The export of capital to Third World countries was considered necessary to provide "an outlet for capital funds which might otherwise be less profitably utilized and an outlet for wartime surplus equipment [which would] aid in the utilization of excess plant capacity."[2]

But internationalists argued that the flow of private capital to the Third World would not take place automatically. Instead the CFR insisted that lending institutions promote foreign investment through strategies that would induce Third World governments to rely on private capital, as opposed to statist options, in developing their economies. On October 11, 1941, CFR members began promoting the establishment of an International Development Authority, described in a way that gave it a resemblance to what later became the World Bank: it was to

guarantee capital invested in backward areas and at the same time establish certain conditions of investment and management. . . . The aim of the plan is to stimulate private investment. . . . If the world's economy is to run at high gear . . . there will have to be a considerable shift in the production pattern of the world, as the primary industries decrease in relative importance. . . . Capitalists tend to invest in the older lines which they know and which are safe. This is exactly what is not wanted, and the IDA can help direct money into new channels. . . . The Authority should not limit itself to saying: "What resources are available in this country? Is it desirable to develop them?" But rather should ask itself: "What will these people want if their living standards rise? Can these needs be economically met by production in

their own country?" . . . The Authority must work within the present system of trade barriers.[3]

There are two primary points that emerge from this description.
First, the CFR was concerned about the tendency for foreign investors
to limit risks to primary product lines such as agribusiness and planta-
tion holdings in Central America and petroleum and minerals in a few
countries in Latin America. Historically, U.S. foreign investments in
Latin America had been dominated by these types of investments. The
CFR was arguing for the importance of expanding foreign investments
to include manufacturing.[4] Second, the CFR contended that foreign
investors should be willing to establish foreign plants or branches that
could take advantage of trade barriers by producing for the local market where necessary and if possible engaging in export-led industrialization in the Third World. The CFR in early 1941 was advocating an
import-substitution industrialization (ISI) strategy for the Third World
as a temporary measure that would allow large manufacturing firms
the option of investing behind trade barriers until conditions became
right for the promotion of export-led industrialization. The CFR understood: "that by accepting industrial enterprises the Authority
might make it possible for one group of American investors to go into
a foreign country and take advantage of tariff walls to take a market
from American exporters. . . . In some cases competition should be
encouraged and in others redundancy should be avoided."[5]

The CFR recognized that "large manufacturing firms would be
most able to take advantage of investment opportunities behind ISI
tariff barriers."[6] The membership of CFR was dominated by these
larger firms, whose members alternated between governmental positions and the private sector after World War II.[7] In a confidential planning document, CFR officials identified three groups of firms based
on their size and relative economic interests in international trade
and investment. The first group included much of the CFR membership, identified as "large manufacturing corporations like General
Motors, United States Steel, General Electric, International Harvester,
etc., interested in foreign plant investment but wishing to export raw
materials, semi-fabricated parts, etc., from this country." The second
category included "an intermediate group comprising the large
export-import houses having substantial capital and considerable experience in the foreign field." The final group was "small businesses
operated with minimum capital and relatively small organiza-

tions, unwilling to assume risk other than the ordinary hazards in doing business inside the United States."[8]

The CFR spoke on behalf of the first group of firms, which were able and willing to invest abroad. The council argued that the American government should use "its best offices to assure . . . development of long-term policies that will justify substantial foreign investment in plant and services."[9] Ideally, the government should "prepare and maintain the ground" for U.S. foreign investment by ensuring that the conditions for such investment, i.e. roads, infrastructure, and the like, are present in the less developed world.[10] There was a recognition that foreign investors would need government assistance to facilitate the movement of capital into the less developed world.

The CFR encouraged the creation of the World Bank in part to facilitate development lending to Third World countries in need of infrastructure that could not be provided by private firms but that was a prerequisite for foreign private investment. Firms represented by the CFR later pushed for increased development assistance through bilateral lending institutions such as the Export-Import Bank. As Robert Wood has argued, Third World countries could turn to EXIM and the World Bank only if private capital was not readily available.[11] Instead of competing with private capital, bilateral and multilateral lending institutions were to provide development lending that would complement and facilitate the flow of foreign investment to the less-developed world.

The CFR pushed for development policies that would open the markets of the advanced industrial countries to exports from the less-developed countries, which would then be able to "repay development loans with new exports, rather than by further restricting imports to the detriment of world trade."[12] The council preferred an ISI strategy that would facilitate a transition to export-led industrialization (ELI), rather than one that would close off Third World markets to U.S. exports. Yet the CFR understood that nationalists in the U.S. were likely to oppose efforts to open U.S. markets fully. The extent to which nationalist firms were successful meant potential problems for an export-led industrialization strategy for the Third World.

An ISI strategy that maintained regional or national tariff barriers was seen as a compromise of benefit to both foreign investors and domestic manufacturers. Maxfield and Nolt sum up the advantages of this strategy for a Republican party consisting of both internationalist and protectionist firms: "Deepening ISI was especially useful for the Republicans because it afforded the opportunity to satisfy simultaneously the internationalist and protectionist wings of the party. ISI policies discouraged manufacturing exports from the Third World to the U.S., while subsidizing U.S. corporations exporting machinery and investing in ISI-protected markets."[13]

Other business groups besides the CFR expressed support for ISI strategies as early as World War II. The National Planning Association (NPA), like the CFR dominated by leaders of the top foreign investors and exporters in the United States, drafted policy recommendations with executive branch officials designed to help provide guidelines for postwar policies toward the Third World. An NPA study from 1939 advocated industrial development in Latin America, supporting the recommendations of the CFR:

It is believed that the investment program in Latin America in the future should not be concentrated on the further specialization of raw materials, but rather should be focused on the development of industries making goods which Latin Americans need, and which would utilize some of the resources now exported. A large variety of products such as clothes, furniture, and construction materials can and should be manufactured and fabricated out of Latin America's own natural resources. Capital for these industries, and for railroads, roads and communication services, and public utilities must come from abroad. . . . Only in this way can the Latin American nations be made sufficiently strong economies so that they will be neither dependent on fluctuating prices in world markets nor on the bargaining power of industrial nations.[14]

Together with the CFR and the NPA, the National Foreign Trade Council (NFTC) and the Committee for Economic Development (CED) represented nearly 10 percent of the 795 largest corporations. The NFTC and the CED also worked closely with government officials in drafting postwar proposals for Third World industrialization. The NFTC in 1943 noted the importance of industrial development in Central and South America:

It is in the best interests of this and all countries to further the industrial expansion of Latin America. . . . In the past less than 10 percent of United States capital invested in Latin America went into manufacturing establishments. Today, tire factories, steel mills, cement factories, textile mills, chemical plants, and the like are wanted. . . . Inequitable measures preventing the transfer of earnings, taxes on the export of capital, too tight immigration laws and curbs on managerial freedom will scare off available capital from this country. . . . We assume that our pre-war markets in such of our specialities as automobiles, farm machinery, electrical devices, office equipment and others . . . will come back to us. What we should be concerned with now is the largely increased market which will come as a result of the era of development in South and Central America which all signs indicate.[15]

Eric Johnston, a president of the Chamber of Commerce, also communicated frequently with State Department officials during and after World War II on behalf of Third World industrialization. In 1945, he argued that using U.S. capital to industrialize the Third World would benefit the U.S. economy by promoting exports of consumer and producer goods.[16] Johnston, along with Walter Salant of the CED, was an ardent proponent of the Point Four program of technical assistance to the Third World.

They envisioned the Point Four program as providing some of the necessary foundations for the expansion of light industry in Central America and elsewhere. Salant insisted that Point Four would provide opportunities for U.S. foreign investors who would be needed to supply the necessary capital for Third World industrialization.[17] As I will document, business internationalists with investments in Latin America supported Point Four, in addition to EXIM and World Bank loans, as part of a "trade not aid" strategy.

Facilitating Direct Foreign Investment

During the 1940s and 1950s, internationalists argued that foreign economic policy toward Latin America should be systematized to facilitate direct foreign investment. The Business Advisory Council (BAC), led by David Rockefeller and established by the Commerce Department in 1950, represented the views of firms with an interest in promoting favorable conditions for foreign investment. At the request of the Commerce Department, the BAC released a summary report in 1952 of its members' views on ways to increase foreign investment.

The survey of BAC members revealed the foremost concerns of leading internationalists regarding U.S. foreign economic policy toward Latin America. First, there was a consensus that aid to Latin America should work to facilitate, not to interfere with, foreign investment opportunities. As David Rockefeller put it in a summary report: "What is important is that public funds through the Export-Import Bank or the International Bank and other forms of aid should not be extended on such terms as to enable Latin American countries to believe that they do not need to take appropriate steps to attract

the much larger volume of private investment that could be available."[18]

Rockefeller, expressing the views of the membership, argued that
public aid must be offered in such a way as to convince Latin American governments of the importance of relying on foreign investment
prior to various forms of public assistance. The BAC argued that
Point Four, the World Bank, and other forms of lending could facilitate foreign investment by providing development assistance for infrastructural projects necessary for private investment but unlikely to
be funded by private investors.[19]

Second, the BAC argued that additional tax incentives for foreign
direct investment were the best means of promotion. At that time,
U.S. corporations with branches abroad were not entitled to defer
taxes on the income of those branches. The BAC pushed for a foreign
economic policy that would allow for such deferral. Other studies led
and staffed by internationalists also advanced tax incentives as part
of their overall recommendations for increasing the rate of foreign
investment abroad: "The Rockefeller Report of 1951 argued that income from foreign sources should be free of United States tax to the
extent necessary to stimulate the flow of private capital to underdeveloped areas. . . . Income from business establishments located
abroad should be taxed only in the country where the income is
earned and should therefore be wholly free of the United States
tax."[20]

The bipartisan Commission on Foreign Economic Policy, chaired
by Clarence Randall of Inland Steel and led by other internationalists,
also recommended that tax incentives be used to encourage private
capital outflows. Internationalists within the CED and the Council on
Foreign Relations had long argued that the availability of public
funds to Third World governments must be limited in order to encourage a reliance on private foreign investment in the development
of industry. Internationalists supported Point Four, EXIM, and the
World Bank as long as their lending policies complemented and encouraged the flow of private investment abroad. As the next section
indicates, the policies of the executive branch during the Truman and
early Eisenhower years largely conformed to the "trade not aid"
strategy outlined by business internationalists.

By the late 1940s and early 1950s, corporate representatives from
the CFR, the NPA, and elsewhere, along with government officials,
hoped that increased foreign direct investment in Latin America
could be achieved through the initiative of private enterprise, the ex-

tension of loans from the World Bank and EXIM, and technical assistance provided through the Point Four program. The fact is that Latin America and other less developed areas took a back seat to the primary efforts to reconstruct Western Europe through the Marshall Plan, which was the focus of U.S. aid efforts in immediately after World War II.

There were other reasons why policy makers targeted relatively minimal aid to Latin America through the early 1950s. Foremost among them, private foreign investment in Latin America was already high in comparison with the levels in other parts of the Third World. Latin America's ability to attract a disproportionate amount of foreign investment without foreign aid was a primary factor in explaining the low level of development assistance offered to the region. In fact, by 1946 and 1947, Latin America accounted for 45.2 percent of total net U.S. direct investment. That figure increased to 50.6 percent between 1948 and 1951. Meanwhile, Latin America received only 0.8 percent of U.S. economic aid between 1948 and 1952.[21]

In the late 1940s and early 1950s, U.S. policy makers emphasized that economic assistance to Latin America would be limited to minimal development programs and technical assistance that would complement and facilitate private foreign investment in the region. Policy makers were careful to structure aid in ways that encouraged reliance on private investment and discouraged statist or nationalist development. Since Latin America was able to attract a significant share of foreign investment without such economic assistance and since policy makers were preoccupied with Western Europe, the Truman and Eisenhower administrations initially opted for a policy of "trade not aid" toward the region.

Truman administration officials agreed that private foreign capital could satisfy the development needs of Latin America. Secretary of State Dean Acheson put forward the rationale for a "trade not aid" strategy by arguing that "it would be contrary to our traditions to place our government's public funds in direct and wasteful competition with private funds. Therefore, it will be our policy, in general, not to extend loans of public funds for projects for which private capital is available."[22]

Policy makers followed this approach in international meetings with Latin American officials. During the Ninth Inter-American Conference at Bogota in 1948, George C. Marshall emphasized that European aid had to take priority over aid to Latin America. Moreover, Marshall argued that Latin America "still had substantial foreign exchange reserves that had been built up during World War II, and an economic aid program was not an urgent necessity."[23] An economic conference promised by Marshall was shelved in light of the low priority given to economic assistance programs to Latin America.

In its first few years in office, the Eisenhower administration also pursued a strategy of "trade not aid." As Joanne Gowa has noted, that approach had the advantage of satisfying both Eisenhower's corporate constituency and his own ideological objectives for a balanced budget: "The tax incentives and the promotion of private capital exports were integral elements of the administration's broader plan to substitute market flows of goods, services, and capital for government aid to economic development abroad. Although the 'trade not aid' strategy derived from the preferences of administration officials for free markets and balanced budgets, it also responded to intense pressure from the private sector to eliminate large governmental capital flows."[24]

The early strategy of "trade not aid" was based on the premise that foreign capital would flow to the Third World even with minimal levels of governmental assistance. In fact, the Rockefeller Report argued that tax incentives, the creation of an International Finance Corporation, and centralization of foreign investment policy under a single agency would be enough to "at least double the present flow of private United States investment to foreign countries, bringing it from one billion to two billion dollars."[25]

An examination of declassified documents from the 1950s reveals that government officials within the Eisenhower administration consistently identified the promotion of foreign direct investment as an important objective of foreign economic policy. In outlining the primary interests of the United States with regard to Latin America, the State Department and the National Security Council both listed the promotion of foreign investment as one of the goals of policy. In a confidential document entitled "United States Relations with Latin America," the State Department outlined the importance of Latin American markets for U.S. companies and the importance of U.S. foreign investment in the region:

In 1950 Latin America purchased about $2.7 billion of United States goods; by comparison, United States exports to Western Europe in the same year were valued at $2.9 billion, only about $200 million more than Latin America—nearly $2 billion of United States exports to Western Europe were financed out of Marshall Plan funds. United States exports to Latin America . . . consist principally of manufactured and semi-manufactured goods.

The region absorbed about 44 percent of our total exports of iron and steel advanced manufactures, 38 percent of our exports of chemicals, 30 percent of our exports of iron and steel products, and 30 percent of our exports of machinery.[26]

The report went on to discuss the importance of foreign investment: "Latin America is . . . important to us as a field of United States foreign investment. At the end of 1950 our direct private investments in the area were about $6 billion compared with direct private investments outside the Western Hemisphere (except Canada) of only $4.6 billion; furthermore, at the unprecedented rate at which dollar investments have flowed to Latin America since the war ($1.7 billion in the three-year period of 1947-1949), it would be reasonable to expect them to continue rapidly to increase."[27]

The expectation during the early years of the Eisenhower administration was that foreign investments would "rapidly increase" without assistance from major aid programs. In fact, as we have seen, aid programs were considered by many internationalists to be a potential hindrance to the expansion of foreign investment.

In a top secret National Security Council (NSC) document, "U.S. Objectives and Courses of Action with Respect to Latin America" (dated March 18, 1953), the NSC reiterated the claim that the promotion of foreign private investment was an important objective of U.S. foreign economic policy toward the region.[28] The document outlined a series of measures to facilitate U.S. investment in line with the "trade not aid" approach that had characterized the policies of the Eisenhower administration.

The NSC report argued that the general policy of the administration should be to "encourage Latin American governments to recognize that the bulk of capital required for their economic development can best be supplied by private enterprise and that their own self-interest requires the creation of a climate which will attract private investment."[29] To achieve a healthy climate for foreign investment, the report continued, efforts should be made to maintain "the present level of International Bank loans and Export-Import Bank loans and, where appropriate, accelerate and increase them, as a necessary supplement to foreign private investment."[30]

The report also emphasized the importance of such economic projects as the Inter-American Highway and the Rama Road in creating the infrastructure for future private investment, in addition to maintaining technical assistance programs through Point Four. Final-

ly, the report noted that the administration should continue to press
for a reduction of U.S. trade barriers that would make "it easy for
Latin American countries to sell their products to us."[31]

In Central America, the World Bank, EXIM, the Point Four program, and other forms of U.S. bilateral aid were used to expedite the
flow of private capital to the region and to discourage statist paths to
development. The following section contrasts the U.S. strategy of
"trade, not aid" with the nationalist proposals of the Economic Commission for Latin America.

"Trade Not Aid" and ECLA

Throughout the early 1950s, the Truman and Eisenhower administrations counterposed their policies of private sector initiative and minimal government assistance against the "statist" policies of the Economic Commission for Latin America (ECLA), a moderate nationalist
organization of Latin American government officials, businessmen,
and middle-class intellectuals. ECLA proposed a world price stabilization scheme, import substitution, and a regional development
bank for the promotion of Latin American economic development.
U.S. officials saw these proposals as obstacles to the U.S. effort to
encourage reliance on private enterprise and minimal state inter-
ference as a path to development.

Prior to 1958, the U.S. government's foreign economic policy was
characterized by opposition to development initiatives from ECLA that
involved increased public funding and statist controls of commodity
prices. U.S. policy makers characterized ECLA's proposals for import-
substituting industrialization as detrimental to U.S. economic interests
in the region. The State Department counterposed private sector initiative against the development planning advocated by ECLA, which was
perceived as limiting the autonomy of U.S. investors and unduly restricting U.S. trade with the region.

U.S. policy makers also opposed the ECLA proposal for a worldwide price stabilization scheme designed to check the downward
fluctuation in the prices of Central American export crops. ECLA and
Latin American nationalists argued that Central American economic
stagnation was largely due to the dependence on a few primary commodities for which prices fluctuated and declined on the world market relative to manufactured goods. Part of ECLA's solution was a
commodity stabilization program to check the downward fluctuation

of commodity prices. The Eisenhower administration rejected a price stabilization program on the grounds that it "would simply shift to this nation [the United States] a large part of the risk for price fluctuations which is not justified by the nature of the problems."[32]

Another issue that separated ECLA and the United States was the proposal for an Inter-American Development Bank. Latin American elites generally supported a regional development bank that would make available long-term, low-interest loans to Latin countries. The United States argued that such a bank would merely compete with private investors by offering public loans on easier terms than were currently available. U.S. policy makers urged continued reliance on the World Bank, EXIM, and Point Four, where assistance programs were designed to complement, not compete with, foreign investment. In a 1954 statement by the administration, U.S. policy makers rejected proposals for a regional development bank for the following reasons: "1) Its legitimate purposes could be handled by either the International Bank for Reconstruction and Development, the Export-Import Bank or private banks, and 2) The United States presumably would have to put up some of the capital for an organization to be run by other countries.[33]

The negative reaction of the Eisenhower administration to proposals for import-substituting industrialization, a price stabilization scheme, and a regional development bank was consistent with the development strategy of "trade not aid" that characterized its lending policies to Central America until the late 1950s. The administration chose to rely on the World Bank, Point Four, EXIM, and foreign investment in its foreign economic program for the region. The next sections examine the multilateral and bilateral lending programs during the "trade, not aid" period.

The World Bank

Internationalists within the CFR, National Planning Association (NPA), and CED helped establish the set of principles that would guide the World Bank in its lending policies toward the Third World. In consultation with government officials, businessmen from leading internationalist organizations urged the U.S. government to support the World Bank's efforts to finance transportation and electrical projects in the Third World as preconditions for foreign investment in light manufacturing. Internationalists insisted that the World Bank should limit its financing to projects that would not otherwise be funded by the private sector but that were necessary for the expansion of foreign investment. In their defense of the fund to fellow internationalists, representatives from the American Bankers Association assured Congress that the World Bank would be a necessary complement to increased U.S. investment in the Third World.[34]

Throughout the 1950s and to the present, the World Bank has engaged in what David Baldwin has referred to as strategic nonlending.[35] Under this development logic, the bank generally has avoided competing with the private sector in its financing efforts. As a result, the majority of the bank's financing is geared toward transportation and electric power projects that facilitate the expansion of private investment. The bank usually leaves the financing of industrial projects to the private sector.

Internationalists interested in expanding the manufacturing investments in the less-developed world hoped that the World Bank, EXIM, and Point Four would help create the preconditions for direct investments in the region during the late 1940s and early 1950s. In the case of Central America, the World Bank followed a fairly typical pattern of lending through the 1950s and 1960s. Early World Bank projects in Central America included the financing of a hydroelectric plant and 375 miles of road in El Salvador, which expanded the opportunities for foreign investment. In Guatemala, the World Bank financed the completion of the Atlantic and Pacific Highways in 1955, after the overthrow of the Arbenz government and the ascendancy to power of the U.S.-backed Armas regime.[36]

Despite these efforts, foreign investors became increasingly convinced that the U.S. government would have to step up its level of foreign assistance if it was to facilitate the growth of a regional market in Central America. In 1955, investors represented by the NPA, the CED, and the CFR pressured the Eisenhower administration to support an International Finance Corporation, an affiliate of the World Bank designed to make loans only to private enterprise without the government guarantees required for World Bank loans. By 1958, the National Planning Association and the Council on Foreign Relations helped draft a Rockefeller Report that called for increased bilateral and multilateral financial support for Central American integration.

Nationalists, however, have been much more skeptical of World Bank programs since their inception and have often sought to block or limit funding. The divisions between internationalists and nationalists were evident during congressional hearings on the proposed creation of the International Development Association (IDA), a soft-loan affiliate of the World Bank. Internationalist organizations such as the CED and NPA supported the creation of the soft-loan institution as a means of enhancing the investment and trade opportunities of American business. Internationalists saw soft loans as a way to increase the spending power of Third World governments, which would then be able to buy more U.S. exports. They also saw soft loans as a means to help finance the infrastructure necessary for profitable American investment.

Nationalists represented by the Chamber of Commerce and the National Association of Manufacturers (NAM) were concerned that the soft-loan institution would substitute public funds for private investment. Internationalists eventually won their case by ensuring nationalists close to Congress that the IDA would be governed by sound banking judgment and fiscally conservative principles in its operating practices.[37]

Nevertheless, nationalists within the Chamber of Commerce and the NAM continued to support cuts in bilateral and multilateral lending programs, especially soft loans, throughout the 1950s and early 1960s.[38] Nationalists also opposed the expansion of bilateral lending to the Third World, including the meager sums provided by the Point Four programs of the late 1940s and early 1950s.

The Point Four Program

During the early 1940s, internationalist businessmen had made clear their interest in promoting industrialization projects in the Third World that would facilitate and increase the level of foreign investment. As was noted earlier, internationalists worked closely with government officials to draft policy recommendations for Third World industrialization. Many of these recommendations were considered and adopted by the Executive Committee on Economic Foreign Policy (ECEFP), an interdepartmental committee including representatives from the Departments of State, Treasury, War, Navy, Interior, Agriculture, Commerce, and Labor, as well as from the Tariff Commission and the Foreign Economic Administration.[39]

The executive committee was formed in 1944 to discuss the outlines of U.S. foreign economic policy in the post-World War II period. The committee stressed that Third World industrialization was essential for promoting U.S. foreign investment and for "providing immediate markets for United States capital goods."[40] The ECEFP also noted that Third World industrialization would provide "an outlet for capital funds which might otherwise be less profitably utilized and [would] make possible the development of export products, thereby creating the means for repayment."[41]

Immediately after World War II, U.S. policy makers focused on the tasks of European reconstruction. By late 1948 and early 1949, however, the State Department had begun to connect the economic vitality of the Third World to the development needs of the United States and Western Europe. The policy makers initially focused on the contributions that Africa, Asia, and Latin America could make toward improving the economies of Western Europe. U.S. officials worried that Western Europe would move toward statist development strategies in lieu of additional markets for their goods.

The economic development of former European colonies and other Third World countries was seen as necessary to provide capital markets that would help ensure both European recovery and additional outlets for U.S. exports. Whether or not this was an accurate view of the economic needs of Europe and the United States mattered less than U.S. policy makers' belief that it was so. As William Mallalieu has noted: "The United States had anticipated that the restoration of Europe would help to bring about economic viability in the rest of the world. It was soon evident, however, that the converse was equally important. The complete success of European plans required progress in the less developed areas of the world. Only increased purchasing power in the underdeveloped countries of Asia, Africa and Latin America could provide adequate markets for European industry."[42]

Both internationalist businessmen and U.S. policy makers supported a technical assistance program for the Third World that would build some of the necessary foundations for economic development. The ECEFP noted the urgency of the matter from the perspective of foreign policy officials: "In the absence of capital exports or continuing gifts from the United States, such a contraction [in world trade] would appear inevitable, because United States imports are unlikely to increase sufficiently to maintain present export levels."[43]

As a result, internationalists close to the Truman administration began to lobby for a technical assistance program that would encourage the development of light industry in Third World countries dependent on only a few agricultural commodities for their foreign exchange. Along with Walter Salant of the CED, the National Planning

Association lobbied for a Point Four program that would facilitate foreign direct investment in the Third World. The NPA "set up a special committee to investigate and publicize the experiences of U.S. companies whose foreign investments complemented Point Four goals."[44] The Business Advisory Council established by the Department of Commerce welcomed the Point Four program for the technical skill it would bring in support of foreign direct investment in the Third World.[45] Leading international investors in Central America, including Rockefeller's International Basic Economy Corporation, the Grace Corporation, International Harvester, American Power and Light, and International Railways of Central America all expressed support for Point Four, stipulating that the program must be designed so as not to compete with private enterprise.[46]

The Point Four program in Central America mirrored the objectives of the program elsewhere: to promote the transition to light industry by pressuring Central American officials to implement favorable tax codes, to eliminate laws discriminating against foreign investment, and to encourage the establishment of industrial development banks as lenders to industrial enterprises.[47]

Point Four Aid to El Salvador

The Point Four program in El Salvador reflected the overall U.S. objectives of promoting government policies conducive to industrial development. Foreign investors viewed El Salvador as one of the best prospects for the development of light industry in Central America. The El Salvadoran government was recognized as one of the most stable bulwarks against communism and left-wing nationalism in the region. U.S. policy makers turned to El Salvador for support during the Guatemalan crisis of 1954, when the United States aided in overthrowing the nationalist government of Arbenz in Guatemala. Prior to that time, U.S. policymakers had sought, through the Point Four program, to encourage a diversification of the Salvadoran economy, away from a strict reliance on coffee and other cash crops toward the development of an infrastructure to serve light industry.

From the beginning, policy makers recognized that the policies favoring industrial development would not be welcomed by all sectors of the Salvadoran elite. Some Salvadoran landowners balked at the notion of using government money for industrial development. In classified State Department documents, U.S. policy makers wrote of the intrasigence of some sectors of the Salvadoran bureaucracy.[48] Yet policy makers were convinced of eventual progress, since Salvadoran President Oscar Osorio and sections of the landowning aristocracy supported investments in light industries and were eager to attract foreign investors.[49]

Confidential memos from State Department officials to Michael J. McDermott, the U.S. ambassador to El Salvador, reveal the aims of U.S. economic assistance. Raymond G. Leddy, assistant secretary of state for inter-American affairs, noted that the Technical Cooperation Administration (initial administrator of the Point Four program) had been increasing its economic assistance to El Salvador with the purpose of "inaugurating an industrial productivity program to assist industrial development, establish new industries, and increase productivity in medium and small industries."[50]

The Point Four program, established in El Salvador in 1952, provided the country with technical specialists and grant assistance in agriculture, health, industry, education, economics, and fisheries. State Department officials noted that the primary aims of the program included providing the Salvadoran government with the skills to develop "individual industrial projects" that would lead to "a notable expansion of industry" by the end of the decade.[51]

The State Department also recognized the importance of agricultural assistance. The Point Four program provided an average of approximately $150,000 per year in grant assistance Salvadoran agriculture between 1953 and 1956, along with eleven technicians and one business manager. The stated aims included "increased production methods through expanded use of insecticides, fungicides, fertilizers, weed killers, defoilants and agricultural machinery."[52] The TCA saw increased agricultural productivity as vital for the development of light industry in El Salvador. Officials believed that higher agricultural output per worker would enhance foreign exchange earnings and release needed capital for industry.[53]

As an expression of the commitment to the development of light industry, the Point Four program channeled an average of $50,000 per year in grant assistance to industrial development. According to internal documents, the primary intent was to provide technical advice to the Salvadoran government and private capital (local and foreign) on ways to "improve industrial productivity and commercial operations."[54] As part of this effort, a U.S. economic adviser, who served as the head of the Point Four field party in El Salvador, advised the Salvadoran government on suitable infrastructure projects. U.S. advisers recognized that the expansion of electrical power and the construction of new roads were essential for the development of light industry.[55]

Point Four officials worked closely with the Salvadoran government in conducting preliminary studies of the completion of the Rio Lempa hydroelectric project, funded with World Bank money beginning in 1949. Leading U.S. investors in Central America welcomed the dam construction as the first step toward increased private investment in El Salvador.[56] *Fortune* magazine noted: "El Salvador must have more electric power; Rio Lempa would meet the need. The establishment of light industries and the expansion of old ones waited on it."[57]

A memo from the State Department's Raymond Leddy to the U.S. ambassador in El Salvador noted that the construction of the hydroelectric project would mean that "individual industrial projects suitable for special assistance would take shape [by 1954] and that some of these [projects] may be of a scale requiring outside financing."[58] The memo went on to add that "while the present TCA training program may appear adequate for immediate needs, a substantial increase in El Salvador's industrial plant next year would create a need for aid which could be channeled into industrial development. Continuous study of El Salvador's industrial potential is made by the IBRD, and it is possible that IBRD or the EXIM bank can assist specific industries."[59]

As part of their effort to enhance the conditions for light industry, Point Four officials worked with the Salvadoran government to devise favorable tax incentives and investment codes for industry. To that end, the Salvadoran government passed the Industrial Promotion Law of 1952, designed to "promote enterprises which, using efficient industrial procedures, devote themselves to the industrial processing of raw materials and the fabrication of primary or semifinished goods into finished products; the preservation and processing of agricultural products; and assembly operations where these involve substantial investment and employment."[60]

The law classified industries into two primary categories, based on whether the industry was new and on the type of goods produced. The industries classified as "new" included those intended to manufacture products not previously produced in El Salvador. Industries classified as "essential" included the production of commodities vital to the lives of Salvadorans, such as food, health items, and shelter.[61] The benefits available included:

1. Exemption from import duties on construction materials.
2. Exemption from duties on machinery, equipment, etc.
3. Exemption from duties on raw materials.
4. Exemption from national and municipal taxes on production and sale of manufactured articles.
5. Exemption from national and municipal taxes on capital invested in the enterprise.[62]

Industries considered both "new" and "essential" were entitled to the highest degree of benefits, including the first three benefits for ten years of operation and the last two benefits for five years, with a further tax exemption of one-half the standard rate for another five years.[63] Other industries were awarded a varied degree of benefits depending on their classification. The TCA evaluated the effectiveness of the Salvadoran law in terms of its usefulness in promoting direct investment and concluded: "It is widely believed that the Law has had a significant effect in stimulating investment in El Salvador. Since 1952, about 225 applicants have been approved [for protection under the law], covering about 100 manufacturing activities. . . . According to official statistics, the total investment by enterprises receiving benefits under the Law from 1952 through 1960 was 173 colones, and the total direct employment generated was 18,000."[64]

Partly as a result of the effectiveness of the law, the State Department consistently gave El Salvador high marks in its country-by-country evaluation of Central America, noting that El Salvador repeatedly set a good example of favorable conditions for profitable foreign investment.[65] In fact, the 1950s was a period of significant industrial growth in El Salvador, the basis for the high growth rates of the 1960s.

Encouraged by the construction of the hydroelectric project and the Industrial Development Law, foreign companies established plants in El Salvador, often in joint ventures with local firms. U.S. investment increased from $18 million in 1950 to $31 million in 1959.[66] Pillsbury began milling imported wheat in El Salvador, Sherwin Williams built a paint plant there, Rockefeller's International Basic Economy Corporation invested in a joint venture with local and Japanese capital, and Pan American built a $3 million dollar hotel-restaurant in San Salvador.[67] Overall, from 1950 to 1956, Salvadoran industrial production increased by 7 percent a year.[68]

However, the Salvadoran market proved to be severely limited in its ability to absorb additional production. Most of the new industries failed to generate sufficient employment to spur consumer demand. Despite the increase in industrial production, consumer goods comprised 75.4 percent of Salvadoran imports in 1951 and 79.7 percent in 1962.[69] The State Department recognized that the economic development of El Salavador was dependent on the creation of a regional infrastructure that allowed for intraregional trade, such as the Inter-American Highway.

U.S. Aid for the Inter-American Highway

In addition to promoting an industrial development law and the Rio Lempa hydroelectric project, the State Department pushed for congressional funds as loans to build the Inter-American Highway system through El Salvador and the rest of Central America. The highway was seen as a prerequisite for viable trading relations among the Central American countries. Most important, policy makers recognized that the highway would give further impetus to light industry by opening markets throughout the Central American region.

In classified documents, policy makers in the State Department defended aid for the highway in two ways: 1) The aid would open up the shipment of manufactures to millions of people throughout Central America. 2) The aid would provide a check against statist development options that might otherwise pose a threat to private investment in the region. An internal memo from Ernest Siracusa, head of Central American and Panamerican Affairs, to Edward G. Miller, the assistant secretary for inter-american affairs, expanded on the first motivation in some detail, noting that the initial military rationale for expenditures on the Inter-American Highway (securing a land route to the Panama Canal) had "given way to economic and political concerns":

Since 1938 U.S. exports to Central America and Panama have increased from approximately $40 million (53 percent of total imports) to approximately $202 million (75 percent of total imports). Allowing for inflation and trade shifts due to the war, much of this increase results from increased income to which the Highway, as has been shown, has made a basic and substantial contribution. A far greater potential for the shipment of manufactures to the nine million people of Central America and Panama, and the receipt therefrom of raw goods, waits upon the further development of these countries. Every penny spent on the Inter-American Highway is not a gift but an investment in the future of our friends and, more importantly, it is an investment in the future needs and markets of the United States.[70]

The memo goes on to emphasize the importance of the Central American market to U.S. manufacturing interests. Siracusa notes that the value of the Central American region for U.S. goods (both exports and direct investments) was in part due to the "high income elasticity of demand for imports" and that: "for every one percent increase in their income, their imports will increase by approximately 3 percent. Accordingly, if the income of the Central American and Panama area should increase by 10 percent in the next 10 years (and the Highway is the kind of investment which makes the greatest single contribution to such growth), total imports, presently around $268 million, may be expected to increase by 30 percent."[71] Such an increase would mean that, based on prevailing levels of U.S. trade, about "75 percent of the increase, or around $60 million, will be supplied by the U.S."[72]

The State Department memo reiterated what had become a common theme in confidential discussions of Central America: that the opening of the region to further foreign investment and trade was a major goal of U.S. foreign economic policy. In addition, Siracusa emphasized the importance of U.S. assistance to prevent any statist development policies that might be adopted in the absence of such aid.

Siracusa put it succinctly: "If grant aid is not available, accelerated road construction (which is vitally needed in this area to achieve the purpose of the foreign aid bill) would be possible only by increased direct taxation, indirect taxation of inflation, and/or by authoritative government controls to force labor and resources into the road project."[73] Thus the aid bill was also designed to help check any trend toward statist development in the region as a whole.

The Inter-American Highway, like the World Bank and Point Four, was designed as part of a "trade not aid" strategy that would lay the foundation for an increase in direct foreign investment. Internationalists supported the creation of the Export-Import Bank as another vehicle to promote increased trade and foreign direct investment in Latin America and the rest of the less developed world.

The Origins and Functions of the EXIM Bank

The American Bankers Association and the National Foreign Trade Council worked with the State Department in drafting plans for the EXIM Bank in the early 1930s. Bankers and manufacturers hoped that

EXIM would enable U.S. producers to increase exports by extending credit and offering financial assistance from the U.S. government. Secretary of State Cordell Hull defended EXIM by noting that without it, "American producers would lose substantial business" to foreign firms whose "governments are . . . giving credit and financial assistance to their commerce."[74]

By the late 1940s, internationalists hoped that EXIM, the World Bank, and Point Four could help pave the way for foreign direct investment in the Third World. Each of these institutions made funds available to Third World governments for infrastructure such as electric power generation and transportation construction, viewed as essential for increased U.S. investment.

Internationalists saw EXIM and the World Bank as complementary to the efforts of U.S. businesses to engage in foreign lending, exporting, and direct investment in the Third World. The EXIM Bank Act of 1945 stipulated one of the major tenets of internationalism: "In the exercise of its functions [the bank] should supplement and encourage, and not compete with, private capital."[75] As Richard Feinberg notes, EXIM has worked with commercial banks in its financial transactions:

Just as EXIM at its inception was responsive to the needs of the private sector for capital, so have its programs adapted to the changing abilities and requirements of the private capital markets. As the capacity of the commercial banks to extend medium- and long-term loans has grown, EXIM has taken them on as co-workers in export finance. Rather than supply 100 percent of the credit itself, EXIM now divides the financial package between itself and commercial lenders. The magnitudes have varied over time, yet during the 1970s the private sector generally covered between 30 and 70 percent of the financial portion of the transaction; this excluded the downpayment, which commercial intermediaries also may have financed.[76]

In addition, EXIM extended risk guarantees to the private banks as an additional incentive for extending loans to foreign buyers of U.S. goods. EXIM covered private banks with a financial guarantee against all commercial and political risks, and "guarantees full repayment of principal and most of interest charges."[77] EXIM helped facilitate the dramatic increases in commercial lending during the 1950s, 1960s and 1970s by easing the financial risks associated with such transactions.

The types of projects financed by EXIM helped both U.S. exporters and direct investors increase their commercial activities in the

Third World. EXIM helped exporters directly by providing a source of credit to foreign buyers of U.S. goods. Most EXIM loans were committed for more than five years, in contrast to the short-term loans preferred by commercial banks for reasons relating to "liability structure, interest-rate fluctuations, uncertainty, flexibility, government regulations, and custom."[78] The loans extended by EXIM were generally for projects that could not easily be financed by Third World governments or the private sector alone.

As Feinberg points out, EXIM also has extended economic and political benefits to foreign-based affiliates of U.S. multinationals. The "fixed interest rates, extended terms and other implicit subsidies" offered to U.S.-based exporters are also available to overseas affiliates.[79] In addition, by providing loans to Third World governments for the purchase of U.S. products, EXIM also has helped promote the types of infrastructure needed for profitable foreign direct investment. Direct investors often wait for the financing of roads, electrical plants, and communications facilities before committing themselves to investments in the Third World. Most loans extended by EXIM are for these types of projects.

In the early 1950s, bankers, direct investors, and exporters pressured the Eisenhower administration for increases in the lending authorizations for EXIM in order to facilitate trade with and investment in the Third World. Business nationalists pressured Congress to limit EXIM authorizations. The resulting battle illustrates the limitations of a "trade, not aid" strategy.

Internationalists vs. Nationalists

The conventional literature dealing with post-World War II foreign economic policy overestimates the degree to which U.S. administrations were able to pursue free trade policies. Studies that focus on the interests of U.S.-as-hegemon in the international arena typically overlook the extent to which domestic actors battled over the terms of foreign economic policy.

One such battle was visible during hearings conducted by Homer E. Capehart, chair of the Senate Banking and Finance Committee, as member of a commission formed to review EXIM lending policies toward Latin America. The Capehart Commission is a useful study of business opinion on foreign economic policy toward Latin America for several reasons. Most important, the Capehart Commission actively sought the opinions of diverse groups of businessmen on questions of foreign lending policies toward Latin America. Capehart organized a Citizens Advisory Committee (CAC) on September 15, 1953, made up of representatives from industry, commerce, and finance. Representatives of the CAC accompanied Capehart on a fourteen-nation tour of Latin America between mid-October and early December 1953. During the tour, the committee interviewed local members of the U.S. Chambers of Commerce, talked with Latin American businessmen and organizations, and reviewed policy differences with government officials in each nation.[80] As one scholar put it: "The most common refrain heard by Capehart [from Latin American public officials] addressed the desire to work with U.S. corporations to import technologies to spur economic development. The major stumbling block, he [Capehart] repeatedly heard, was inadequate financing which Latin Americans need to buy big ticket items."[81]

In a report summarizing the economic development needs of Latin America on a country-by-country basis, the Capehart Commission concluded that the extension of loans and credits by EXIM should be increased to allow for the construction of economic development projects built and operated with U.S. capital.[82] Senator Capehart echoed the concerns of internationalists by noting that the continued stability of the U.S. economy was in part dependent on the economic health and spending power of Third World nations.

He also insisted that the results of the study indicated that without increased bilateral assistance, Latin American governments were more likely to adopt statist solutions to their development problems, thereby shutting out U.S. capital in favor of Soviet-style planning. The lending policies of EXIM had the advantage of tying loans to purchases of U.S. goods and services, thereby assuring that development projects were "hammered out according to businesslike criteria between Latin American governments and/or firms and U.S. corporations."[83] EXIM lending also was seen as promoting social stability: "Money invested in wealth-creating ventures on a long-term credit basis will enable the economies of other countries to expand, will provide greater employment opportunities, raise wages and living standards, and wipe out illiteracy, disease and social discontent."[84]

Internationalists lobbied Congress for increases in EXIM lending. The lobbying efforts were especially pronounced during hearings held by the Banking and Finance Committee in January and in June

of 1954. At the hearings, internationalists sought to counter the nationalist sentiment of domestic industry and small business, which
lined up to oppose increased EXIM lending.

Internationalists in the Business Advisory Council and the Rockefeller Commission had long argued that EXIM lending should be
increased, only to discover that protectionists within the Eisenhower
administration, led by Secretary of the Treasury George Humphrey,
had successfully maneuvered to lower EXIM lending significantly.
Humphrey, supported by protectionist businessmen in the textile,
watchmaking, sugar, and beet industries and by some exporters be-
set by international competition, had used his control over foreign
economic policy to reduce EXIM loans to Latin America from $147
million in 1952 to only $7.6 million in 1953.[85]

Humphrey was able to push through cuts in EXIM lending after
Congress approved a reorganization of the bank on April 30, 1953.
The reorganization plan gave the Treasury Department virtual control over the day-to-day policies of EXIM by removing the bank from
the supervision of the National Advisory Council, which had previously ensured that the State Department could select one member of
the board of directors. Under the reorganization, the State Department no longer had any real control over EXIM lending.

Internationalist businessmen were alarmed by the dramatic cuts
in EXIM lending. As early as 1951, the Rockefeller Report proposed
the centralization of foreign economic policy under the primary direction of the State Department. As part of this recommendation, the
report argued for the creation of an assistant administrator of private
enterprise, whose primary responsibility would be to facilitate private
investment abroad by coordinating the lending policies of the EXIM
Bank.

The internationalists behind the Rockefeller Report hoped this
proposal would allow for increased lending by EXIM as part of a con-
certed effort to promote foreign direct investment. In fact, much of the
Rockefeller Report concentrated on ways to increase the level of foreign investment abroad, including the expansion of EXIM and World
Bank lending and the creation of an Investment Finance Corporation.

As we have seen, President Eisenhower was also concerned
about increasing the rate of foreign direct investment abroad. But he
agreed with Republicans such as Humphrey that a "trade not aid"
strategy must seek to encourage capital flows without much government assistance. Eisenhower hoped that foreign investors would in-

crease their rate of investment in the Third World without large amounts of government aid.

Humphrey had convinced Eisenhower by 1953 of the necessity of reorganizing EXIM Bank policies under the direction of Treasury, which could then limit EXIM lending in the interests of prudent fiscal policies. Humphrey also believed in the importance of furthering foreign direct investment, but he insisted that government efforts should be limited to obtaining favorable treatment for U.S. investors, "including the establishment of convertibility, political stability, and freedom from unreasonable discrimination."[86]

In this political context, internationalists within the Randall Commission and the Capehart Commission were concerned in 1954 with two primary tasks: (1) pressuring Congress and the administration into supporting higher levels of EXIM lending for the Third World, and (2) reducing the barriers to trade within the United States that hampered efforts of foreign investors to pursue a strategy of export-led industrialization in the Third World.

The first task proved easier than the second. By the end of the Capehart Commission, internationalists had succeeded in securing increases in EXIM lending over the objections of nationalists and in returning control of EXIM to the National Advisory Committee, thereby reducing Humphey's control over EXIM. On June 11, 1954, Capehart introduced Senate Bill 3589 to liberalize EXIM lending practices. The act reestablished an independent board of directors and increased the bank's lending authority by $500 million.

However, efforts to liberalize U.S. trade policy were less successful. Internationalists close to the Eisenhower administration, specifically the Business Advisory Council, had long argued for a reduction in tariffs that would facilitate imports from foreign-owned industries in the Third World.[87] In his State of the Union Message in 1953, Eisenhower pushed for an extension of the Reciprocal Trade Agreements Act. The act "granted the President a three-year period in which to negotiate reciprocal trade agreements with other countries, agreements that could lower tariffs by as much as 50 percent."[88] Eisenhower initially called for a three-year extension of the act, along with the authority to make additional tariff cuts. Nationalists within the Republican party attacked the measure as potentially catastrophic for the interests of domestic manufacturers.

The nationwide Committee of Industry, Agriculture and Labor on Import-Export Policy was formed in 1953 to lead a campaign against tariff liberalization. Led by the National Coal Association, the National Chemists Association, and companies involved in textile, watchmaking, sugar, and beet production, as well as lead and zinc producers, the group succeeded in pressuring the Eisenhower administration to limit the proposed extension of the trade act to one year. As a further concession to its nationalist wing, the Eisenhower administration agreed not to negotiate any major trade deals that year.[89]

The nationalists also succeeded in maintaining the legislation's "peril point" and "escape clause" provisions, which limited the President's authority in reducing tariffs.[90] The peril point clause required the Tariff Commission to establish a limit beyond which a tariff rate cut would be considered a threat to domestic industry. The escape clause allowed the United States to withdraw from a reciprocal trade agreement in the event that "unforeseen developments" had hurt domestic industry.[91]

Internationalists within the Committee for Economic Development, the Council on Foreign Relations, the National Planning Association, and the National Foreign Trade Council worked with governmental officials to devise a "trade not aid" strategy for Latin America and elsewhere in the less developed world during the 1940s and early 1950s. The goals of the strategy were to promote the conditions necessary for an increase in foreign direct investment in Third World countries.

The strategies were pursued by business internationalists and their allies in the State Department and Congress. First, business organizations and government officials worked together to draft and implement aid programs financed by the World Bank, Point Four, and EXIM. Aid was designed to complement, not compete with, foreign direct investment. Second, business internationalists and the State Department attempted to lower U.S. barriers to trade as a way to promote export-led industrialization in the less developed world.

Business internationalists succeeded in increasing the level of EXIM lending and in securing the creation of the Investment Finance Corporation by 1955. However, business nationalists successfully blocked efforts to liberalize significantly U.S. barriers to foreign trade. As a result, the practical difficulties of promoting export-led industrialization for the Third World began to mount.

Most important, business internationalists and executive branch policy makers were becoming concerned that the level of foreign aid was too low to achieve the preconditions for the desired level of foreign direct investment. As I will document in chapter 3, by the mid-1950s U.S. investors were pressuring executive branch officials to shift from "trade not aid" to "trade and aid" as a way to facilitate increased foreign investment in the less developed world.

The shift to "trade and aid" was complicated by the opposition of business nationalists to any foreign aid that would benefit their economic competitors abroad. However, business internationalists were often able to win increases in foreign aid under conditions of tight bipolarity, or heightened global competition with the Soviet Union. In the case of Guatemala, internationalists were able to convince nationalists of the importance of raising the level of foreign aid to counter the "Soviet threat" to the hemisphere. As a result, increased foreign aid to Guatemala became the precursor of a trade-and-aid approach to Latin American development.

The trade-and-aid approach reached its zenith during the Kennedy administration's Alliance for Progress. As I will document in chapter 4, the Kennedy White House and the State Department worked with business internationalists to expand foreign assistance to Latin America dramatically. Most notably, the administration provided direction and assistance for the creation of the Central American Common Market. The CACM was created as a vehicle for import-substituting industrialization in Central America. U.S. direct investors saw the CACM as ideal for increasing their manufacturing investments in the region.

3

U.S. Intervention in Guatemala: Prelude to a Common Market

The move by the Eisenhower administration from "trade not aid" to "trade and aid" was a gradual shift as policy makers recognized the limitations of the "trade not aid" strategy. As early as July 23, 1953, when the administration was still pursuing a "trade not aid" approach, the National Security Council issued a policy statement (NSC 144/1) warning of the difficulties of raising foreign direct investment in Latin America absent higher levels of government assistance.[1]

The NSC report discussed the potentially negative effects of a reduction in EXIM lending for private investment in the region. In addition, the report urged stronger lobbying efforts to check the influence of nationalists in Congress who had succeeded in maintaining significantly high quotas on lead and zinc products imported from Latin America.

By 1954-55, a series of corporate reports had expressed concerns about the difficulties of facilitating the development of private and foreign capital in the Third World. Despite the success of the executive branch in overturning the reduction in EXIM lending to the Third World, corporate elites and policy makers within the Eisenhower administration expressed the opinion that the administration would have to expand its lending efforts if it was to encourage higher levels of U.S. investment abroad.

A planning study released by the National Planning Association in 1955 urged the Eisenhower administration to develop a foreign economic policy that would serve to "induce as many as possible of the underdeveloped countries to help mitigate the factors now making the climate for private foreign investment so unfavorable."[2] According to the NPA study, the U.S. government should provide additional investment funds "needed to supplement private foreign investment and to make possible necessary projects outside the range of private interests."[3]

The NPA urged the U.S. government to increase its efforts to promote the development of transportation, port and power facilities, water control, public health improvements, and other progress needed to attract private capital investment in the Third World.[4] In addition, the NPA study supported the establishment of an Investment Development Corporation, "empowered not only to provide venture capital to private enterprises, but also to investigate investment opportunities, set up projects on its own account, and manage them during their initial stages until they could be sold to private investors." The Development Corporation would "provide a new source of venture capital and open up new opportunities for private investors."[5] The details of the NPA study were presented to the U.S. Council on Foreign Economic Policy, a government body composed of the director of the Federal Operations Administration, the secretaries of state, treasury, commerce, and agriculture, their principal deputies, and White House staff members.

In addition to the NPA, other internationalists close to the Eisenhower administration articulated their support for increased government lending to the Third World as a way to encourage direct foreign investment. C.D. Jackson, vice-president of Time-Life Books and long-time member of the Committee for Economic Development, cited a study by Walt Rostow and Max Millikan, two professors from the Massachusetts Institute of Technology, in defense of the urgency of increased government loans to the Third World. In correspondence from Jackson to Secretary of State John Foster Dulles, Jackson made repeated reference to the Rostow-Millikan study as a rationale for increased foreign assistance.[6]

The Rostow-Millikan study was made available to the U.S. Council on Foreign Economic Policy on November 24, 1954. In the study, the professors warned of a "capital shortage" in the Third World that made industrialization difficult to achieve. The authors urged the creation of an international lending agency that could provide "additional capital imports of about $3.8 billion per annum" for a decade to the undeveloped portions of the "free world."[7] Rostow and Millikan provided the following breakdown of estimates for regional lending: South Central Asia, $1 billion; rest of Asia, $1 billion; Middle East, $0.5 billion; Latin America, $1 billion; and Africa $0.3 billion.[8]

Jackson expanded upon the recommendations of Rostow and Millikan in promoting what he called a New World Economic Policy to address the problems faced by Third World countries in lieu of foreign capital investment. Jackson argued that the maintenance of the U.S. "way of life" was dependent on the economic growth and prosperity of the underdeveloped countries. He insisted that "to stay free and prosper with us, the industrializing trading countries, especially Germany and Japan, will need the assurance of expanding markets not now in sight; and the underdeveloped countries will need more evidence of the superiority of freedom over Communism as an environment for economic growth."[9]

Here Jackson echoed the arguments developed by the Committee for Economic Development, the Council on Foreign Relations, and the National Planning Association about the importance of the Third World to the economic vitality of the advanced industrial countries.[10] Jackson and other internationalists continued to argue for a foreign economic policy that would facilitate direct foreign investment, on the basis of both the increased markets that the Third World would provide and the increased production that would be made possible.[11]

Jackson proposed three primary measures as part of his New World Economic Policy for the Third World. The first was the creation of an international loan fund designed to "eliminate capital shortage as an obstacle to growth."[12] The loan fund would make available $20 billion over five years, with the U.S. supplying $10 billion, or $2 billion a year, and the rest supplied by other industrial countries. The fund would make loans to Third World countries based on "businesslike criteria," and its objectives were to include increasing the real incomes of the underdeveloped countries by a preliminary rate of 1 percent per capita a year and encouraging a larger flow of international private capital to the Third World.[13]

The second measure centered on increasing the technical knowledge of developing countries to ensure that capital was used effectively. This meant increasing U.S. technical assistance programs like Point Four and similar United Nations programs to include "more scientific aid and more industrial and management techniques."[14] The third measure focused on improving trading relations between the First and Third World by encouraging trade liberalization and tariff reductions and by "ceasing to insist that U.S. loans and grants be spent directly on U.S. goods."[15] Jackson echoed the NPA report in calling for commodity agreements with the Third World that would help stabilize raw materials markets by means of an "expanded stock-piling" program.[16]

The Council on Foreign Relations also promoted a shift from a "trade not aid" to a "trade and aid" strategy by 1954. Eugene Staley's *The Future of Underdeveloped Countries* was the most extensive and influential council publication to elaborate the importance of a "trade and aid" strategy for the underdeveloped world. In internal documents, State Department policy makers referred to the publication as evidence for the urgency of adopting a "trade and aid" approach.[17] Policy makers concerned about the lack of opportunities for foreign investment in underdeveloped countries examined the council publication for recommendations on ways to improve the investment climate. The sections of the book dealing with foreign aid succinctly state the concerns of leading internationalists regarding the importance of a "trade and aid" strategy:

The "trade not aid" slogan is much less applicable to the underdeveloped countries than to Europe. Now that the European countries, with the aid of the Marshall Plan, have recovered their war-damaged productive capacities they are in a position to pay for their own import needs, if only they can find receptive markets in which to sell their export goods. Europe has a large installed capacity of modern factories and farms, with the skills, organization, transportation and communication equipment, educational and health services, and the other facilities needed to operate them. In the underdeveloped countries all these things have to be created. Their problem is not merely to market the output of existing productive capacity and to achieve a gradual expansion. It is rather to increase that productive capacity radically. . . . The more realistic slogan to apply to most underdeveloped countries is "trade and aid."[18]

The council publication went on to emphasize that increased foreign aid was essential to create the preconditions for further foreign investment. The problem faced by most Third World countries was a lack of capital that impeded investment opportunities and the development of industry. A major goal of the council was to find ways to improve the "climate which private capital needs in order to function effectively," including such "basic utilities as education, public health, reasonably good administration, roads, irrigation, and agricultural extension services."[19]

The conclusion was that these needs must be met "through public administration and by public investment."[20] Absent such public assistance, "neither local nor foreign private enterprise will be able to take hold effectively in other segments of the economy."[21] It was recommended that a special international fund be created "to make loans at low interest rates or outright grants for essential projects of economic development that cannot be financed by private investment or on regular banking principles."[22] Extension of foreign aid was seen as essential in order to ease the risks associated with private investment in underdeveloped countries. To the extent that government aid is successful, "the risks which discourage investors will gradually decline and private capital can begin to carry a larger share of the load."[23]

Internationalists represented by the CED, the CFR, and the NPA pressured the Eisenhower administration to increase foreign assistance to the Third World so as to facilitate increased foreign investment and trade. These organizations made three recommendations for increasing foreign aid: 1) Increase the disbursements of the Export-Import Bank and the World Bank. 2) Create an International Finance Corporation to make loans in local foreign currencies to private investors without government guaranty. 3) Create a Development Loan Fund to channel needed capital to the Third World at easier terms than were then available from the World Bank and EXIM.

These recommendations were articulated to the administation through study groups, commissions, and reports sponsored by internationalist organizations. The Eisenhower administration responded by pressuring Congress to increase the disbursements for the EXIM bank and the World Bank.[24] As we have seen in chapter 2, the administration won congressional authorization for increases in EXIM funding despite the opposition of nationalists in Congress. In addition, the administration successfully promoted the creation of the International Finance Corporation in 1955 as part of the World Bank.

Despite these moves toward a "trade and aid" posture, the administration failed to satisfy internationalists within the CED, the NPA, and the CFR who were calling for the creation of a development loan fund that would make possible a substantial increase in the disbursements to the Third World. The Eisenhower administration was unwilling in 1955 to push for the creation of a development loan fund,[25] partly because of the battle between internationalists and nationalists within the Republican party.

Business Conflict over "Trade and Aid"

The Republican party during the Eisenhower administration included both internationalists and nationalists in its constituency. The strategy of "trade not aid" had been based on a recognition that nationalists within the party would oppose high levels of foreign assistance to the Third World. As we have seen, Eisenhower initially hoped to promote foreign investment through minimal foreign assistance, provided by EXIM, and through programs such as the foreign investment tax credit.

Yet even these minimal efforts to promote foreign investment met with resistance from nationalist groups in Congress, who succeeded in blocking the foreign investment tax credit and limiting EXIM disbursements in 1953. Nationalists were also successful in maintaining limitations on the Reciprocal Trade Act, thereby limiting the authority of the Eisenhower administration to reduce tariff barriers unilaterally.

Given this political climate, the administration was unwilling and unable to go very far in promoting a "trade and aid" approach. In fact, the administration still hoped by 1955 that minimal increases in foreign lending would be sufficient to encourage the appropriate levels of foreign investment. A confidential report from the undersecretary of state on EXIM bank policy in Latin America, released in March 1955, spelled out the major aims and assumptions of U.S. lending policy toward Latin America. The report indicated that a major goal of lending institutions was to make possible increased U.S. investment in Latin America.[26] With that goal in mind, the document indicated that EXIM disbursements for Latin America should be stepped up from $110 million per year in 1955 to $200 million per year by 1958 and that World Bank disbursements should be stepped up from $69 million to about $100 million per year in the same period.[27]

These figures fell as much as $300 million to $400 million short of the targets proposed by leading internationalists close to the administration.[28] Still, the National Security Council felt that such increases would be sufficient to achieve the goal of increasing U.S. direct private investment in the region. According to the report, "This level of public funds will do the job upon the assumption that United States direct private investment in Latin America will step up from $275 million in 1954 to the annual rate of about $400 million that it has averaged over the post-war period."[29]

The report added that the "most effective way to stimulate this highly desirable flow of private capital is through providing tax incentives to such investment."[30] In addition, it was proposed that an Investment Finance Corporation be created as part of the World Bank. The report also encouraged the administration to press Congress for liberalized trade barriers to facilitate the sale of Latin American goods to the U.S. Finally, the report called for the continuation of technical assistance programs to the region.

What was the primary reason for the slow response of the administration to internationalist pressure to dramatically increase foreign assistance to Latin America and the rest of the Third World? The most important political obstacle remained the nationalist bloc within the Republican party, which continued to lobby Congress for limitations on foreign assistance and stiffer protectionist measures on behalf of domestic industry. Nationalists were well represented in the influential Hoover Commission Reports, compiled by businessmen and academics assigned to make recommendations to the executive branch concerning its funding priorities and organizational requirements.

In June 1955, the Hoover Commission released a report on overseas economic operations that represented a stark contrast to the recommendations of internationalists. The commission was highly critical of foreign lending programs to the less-developed world, recommending reductions in the level of U.S. technical assistance programs to facilitate more reliance on local administrators and less on U.S. technicians.[31] The commission also warned against "embarking upon ambitious projects [for the Third World] on the basis of no more than the general desire to industrialize and with astonishingly inadequate information concerning all the relevant technical, social and economic data upon which success of the project so greatly depends."[32] Unlike the international investors, who wanted to expand foreign assistance to facilitate increased manufacturing production in the Third World, the Hoover Commission argued that foreign aid should be shifted away from industrial promotion and toward "agricultural improvements and irrigation projects."[33]

The Hoover Commission members were ideological nationalists who were skeptical of, and often opposed to, increased foreign aid. Their primary concern was to minimize government expenditures on foreign aid programs that they considered wasteful and harmful to the domestic economy. Most important, they did not support foreign aid that served to benefit international manufacturers, who would then be in a better position to compete with domestic U.S. industry. A majority statement released by the commission in June 1955 summarized its general view toward foreign aid: "Since the end of World War II, the United States has spent more than $50 billion in foreign aid. . . . Surely, after almost 10 years, the time has come to apply some brakes to this overseas spending program. We believe, therefore, that the Commission should recommend substantial reductions in expenditures for this purpose. By no other means will the growing trend toward permanent foreign spending be halted.[34]

Secretary of the Treasury George Humphrey was close to this nationalist bloc on questions of limiting foreign aid, and he succeeded for a time in substantially limiting the development assistance levels of EXIM. In addition, nationalists in Congress succeeded in blocking administration efforts to secure a foreign investment tax credit.

In the midst of this internal dissent within the President's own party, the Eisenhower administration could move at only a slow pace in the transition from "trade not aid" to "trade and aid." Even the moves of the administration to promote the Investment Finance Corporation were handicapped by the opposition of members of Congress and influential nationalist businessmen, with one opponent of the IFC expressing the sentiment of the Republican opposition by stating that "the IFC was wrong in principle and dangerous in practice."[35] The result of business opposition meant compromise between internationalists and nationalists over the final terms of the IFC, lowering its capital from $400 million to $100 million and authorizating only $35 million by the U.S. Congress as the nation's subscription to the corporation's fund.[36]

In this context, business internationalists were ultimately able to win substantial increases in foreign assistance only under conditions of tight bipolarity, or heightened competition between the United States and the former Soviet Union. The case of Guatemala is an early example of a shift to a "trade and aid" strategy desired by internationalists.

Corporate Interests in Guatemala

Internationalists pressured the administration to intervene in Guatemala to stabilize the investment climate and to promote the creation of institutional channels that would allow for an expansion of U.S. aid to the region. Internationalists saw Guatemala as a potential showcase for aid programs designed to increase the opportunities for profitable investment in Central America. After the U.S.-backed coup of 1954, internationalists pressured the Eisenhower administration to dramatically increase the flow of aid to the country. In many ways, the creation of aid programs for Guatemala became a necessary prelude for the more ambitious lending schemes of the Central American Common Market and the Alliance for Progress.

In order to achieve their objectives in Guatemala, internationalists had to convince the Eisenhower administration to use its economic and political clout to overthrow a reformist government and to
implement aid programs that would facilitate further U.S. investment
opportunities. The internationalists were successful because they
were well represented within influential corporate bodies close to the
administration, such as the CFR, CED, and NPA, and because the
Eisenhower administration shared a commitment to promoting increased U.S. investment in the region.

In the case of Guatemala, U.S. investors had long dominated the
economic and political affairs of the country without significant challenge. However, the rise of the reformist governments of Juan José
Arevalo and Jacob Arbenz (1944-54) soon posed a significant threat to
the ambitions of the Eisenhower administration for increased U.S.
direct investment in the region. It was in this context that the administration, responding to pressure from leading international investors
to expand the level of U.S. government assistance in order to stabilize
the investment climate in Guatemala, overthrew the Arbenz government and pressured the postcoup regime to implement a series of
reforms designed to attract U.S. capital to the region.

The importance of United Fruit, International Railways of Central
America, and Empressa Electrica to the foreign economic policy of the
Eisenhower administration is reflected both in the sheer economic
scale of their operations in Guatemala and in their regular access to key
officials within the Eisenhower administration.[37] United Fruit was the
single largest investor in Guatemala, its annual profit exceeding $65
million by 1950.[38] The corporation, which exported almost one-third of
all the bananas shipped from Latin America to the United States, was
the "leading banana grower in every Central American and Caribbean
country."[39] United Fruit derived approximately 25 percent of its overall earnings from its Guatemalan operation.

Second only to United Fruit (and partially owned by United
Fruit) was International Railways of Central America (IRCA), a New
Jersey corporation that provided "all of Guatemala's railway facilities
except an insignificant government line 20 miles long, and about 200
miles of trackage owned by United Fruit which is used by IRCA under contractual agreement between the two companies."[40] The IRCA
line ran "from Puerto Barrios, on the Caribbean coast, through Guatemala City to Ayulta on the Mexican border near the Pacific Coast,
with a main branch also connecting with San Jose, on the Pacific
Coast," while another branch reached San Salvador.[41]

Empressa Electrica, owned by American and Foreign Power Co., was the third largest investor in Guatemala, with investments in excess of $12 million. By 1953, Empressa Electrica supplied electrical energy to more than 40,000 residential, commercial, and industrial customers located in Guatemala City and nearby towns.[42]

Overall, U.S. private investment in Guatemala had increased from $6 million in 1897 to close to $59 million by the beginning of the Depression, with the bulk of the increase accounted for by United Fruit, IRCA, and Empressa Electrica.[43] In addition, Pan American Airways, W.R. Grace and Co., and "a number of smaller investors in mining and foreign telecommunications entered the Guatemalan market" in the 1930s looking for "moneymaking outlets for their capital."[44]

By the 1940s, U.S. investors in Guatemala had grown accustomed to favorable treatment from Guatemalan governments. U.S. administrations had long supported repressive Guatemalan governments on the grounds that they protected U.S. interests in the region. Richard Immerman succinctly describes the role played by Guatemalan dictator Jorge Ubico in protecting U.S. "interests" from 1931 to 1944:

Through its courtship of United Fruit, the Ubico regime demonstrated that Guatemala provided opportunities, with its orderly and tranquil political situation and its cheap and docile work force. Ubico granted so many monopolies that, by the time of the 1944 revolution, United States companies virtually dictated Guatemala's economic life. In addition to the previously mentioned monopolies of the country's transportation and power systems [not to mention United Fruit's influence on agricultural jobs], United States interests controlled the airways, the communications networks, such recreational activities as movies, and even a large portion of the press. When the revolutionary junta took over at the end of 1944, investments had reached ninety to one hundred million dollars.[45]

The Truman administration indicated its commitment to protecting U.S. investments in Guatemala in a 1949 memorandum from the assistant secretary of state. U.S. companies also communicated regularly with the Eisenhower administration about the policies of the governments of Arevalo and Arbenz.

The Eisenhower administration responded with a clear indication of its commitment to protect U.S. investors in Guatemala, which it considered equivalent to U.S. "interests" in the country. In a secret document prepared by the Office of Middle American Affairs, American "interests" in Guatemala were defined as the "United Fruit Company, International Railways of Central America and Empressa

Electrica."[46] The document focused on the economic threats to these companies, including the "seizure of three-fourths of the Fruit Company's land, the "embargo . . . placed on [the] property" of IRCA, and the development of a hydroelectric power station by the Guatemalan government that "takes water from the river supplying two of [Empressa Electrica's] plants."[47]

Leading U.S. investors pressured the Eisenhower administration to intervene against the policies of the Arbenz government, which were thought to set a bad example for other governments in the region. These investors' success in influencing the administration to intervene was an indication of their relative influence with key administration officials. The Eisenhower administration was dominated by officials with links to international corporate bodies that sought to increase the level of U.S. direct investment in manufacturing industries in the Third World (see chap. 2). The administration's quick response in part reflected the threat that the Guatemalan government posed to ongoing U.S. efforts to expand U.S. investments in Central America.

United Fruit, Empressa Electrica, and IRCA complained to the Eisenhower administration about the efforts of the Arbenz government to establish economic competitors that could threaten the monopoly position of U.S. interests within the limited domestic market.[48] The Arbenz government had moved to establish a new Atlantic port to compete with United Fruit's Puerto Barrios, an Atlantic highway competitive with IRCA, and a government-run hydroelectric plant that "would provide cheaper and better service" than Empressa Electrica.

In undertaking these measures, the Arbenz government was embarking on a program to enable Guatemalan capitalists to compete with foreign firms. Contrary to public rhetoric about the Guatemalan government being controlled by communists seeking Soviet-led expansion throughout the hemisphere, internationalists in internal documents cited efforts of the Guatemalan government to expand capitalist competition with U.S. monopolies as a primary concern.

The government of Jacob Arbenz was not dominated by communists, but Arbenz did legalize the Communist party and he relied on communists influential within the trade unions for support for government policies. After 1952, U.S. firms were especially concerned about worker and peasant mobilizations that were thought to be encouraged by the policies of the Arbenz government. IRCA complained to U.S. officials when the Guatemalan government used an "intervenor" to direct the affairs of the company following a strike in April of 1954.[49] United Fruit also complained of strike waves that threatened to disrupt its operations and cut into its profits.[50] Each company blamed the policies of the Guatemalan government for stirring up worker unrest in the country. In fact, U.S. companies consistently equated worker efforts to take advantage of their newly won right to organize (as of 1947) as another indication of the negative effects of Guatemalan communism.

Internationalists pressured the Eisenhower administration to intervene in Guatemala to promote the conditions for profitable investment that had existed prior to the Arevalo and Arbenz governments. U.S. investors close to the Eisenhower administration saw the Guatemalan government as an obstacle to the expansion of investments in the region. After the U.S.-backed coup of 1954, internationalists succeeded in pressuring the administration to establish the institutional channels for increased U.S. aid to Guatemala.

As noted earlier, however, domestic industrialists and exporters with minimal direct foreign investment, also influential within the Republican party, succeeded in limiting the Eisenhower administration's attempts to promote direct foreign investment abroad. This conservative wing of the Republican party wanted to maintain a "trade not aid" strategy toward the Third World and generally opposed expansion of foreign lending programs. To achieve their objectives in Guatemala, internationalists had to convince nationalists influential within Congress that the Guatemalan situation required U.S. intervention to protect "national security" interests.

Public Anticommunism and Private Interests

U.S. direct investors in Guatemala convinced nationalists to support U.S. intervention by appealing to their ideological opposition to communism. In public documents, internationalist business groups played down the economic motivations for U.S. intervention in favor of a generalized anticommunist rhetoric. Despite different economic interests, domestic industrialists shared an ideological opposition to communism that characterized the cold war period. To secure political and economic assistance to bolster their investment opportunities in Guatemala, internationalists recognized that they would have to convince Congress that the Guatemalan government represented a communist threat to U.S. national security interests in the Western Hemisphere.

Essentially, internationalists employed different rhetoric when communicating with Congress and the U.S. public than they did when communicating with the Eisenhower administration. In public documents, internationalists emphasized the communist threat posed by the Guatemalan government, a threat that transcended the economic interests of U.S. corporations. In private documents, internationalists pressured the Eisenhower administration to intervene in Guatemala for the purpose of protecting U.S. investors in the country.

The public effort included a massive lobbying campaign led by United Fruit and orchestrated by public relations specialist Edward Bernays. As noted by Bernays in his autobiography, one aspect of the lobbying effort was a media blitz designed to convince the U.S. public that the United Fruit Company was the "most enlightened and progressive employer in Central America."[51] United Fruit paid the expenses for several prominent journalists to travel to Central America and report on the actions of the Guatemalan government. The result was several articles in *Life* magazine and the *New York Times* critical of the communist leanings of the Arbenz government.[52] An article in the *New York Times* dated September 1, 1953, entitled "How Communism Won Control in Guatemala," referred to the Guatemalan government as "fellow-travelling."[53]

The themes of this public campaign were that Guatemala had become a base for an international communist conspiracy controlled by the Soviet Union and that communists were using Guatemala as a staging ground for a takeover of the entire hemisphere. From the late 1940s to 1954, articles critical of the communist leanings of the Guatemalan government appeared in *Reader's Digest*, the *New York Herald Tribune*, the *Chicago Tribune*, the *Saturday Evening Post*, and reports of the major wire services.[54] As one prominent U.S. diplomat pointed out, the coverage of Guatemala during this period far exceeded any previous attention paid to the small Central American country:

The campaign against Guatemala is too unanimous to have come about by mere chance. *Reader's Digest* and several other of the largest publications in the U.S. reach a total of about 40 million readers. These are joined by hundreds of smaller papers in this country, all of them indicting Guatemala as the greatest center of anti-democratic strength on this side of the Iron Curtain. All this, backed by prominent members of Congress, does not come about without some planning—especially concerning a small Latin American country, usually rating a dozen small items a year in the metropolitan press.[55]

In addition to the media campaign, United Fruit relied on corporate organizations such as the National Planning Association and the Council on Foreign Relations to rally support from Congress and the public for U.S. intervention in Guatemala. In 1953, the NPA published a study, "Communism versus Progress in Guatemala," which sought to win public support for U.S. intervention. The study argued that the Communist party of Guatemala was "a working arm of Soviet imperialism" and had become "the most powerful active influence in Guatemalan life."[56] Rejecting the notion of any significant popular support for the Arbenz government, the report argued that the government was dominated by Soviet-backed Communists who had been able "to infiltrate positions of power out of all proportion to their numbers and degree of popular support."[57]

The sponsors of the study had ties to the CFR and policy makers within the Eisenhower administration. Nine CFR members were represented on the committee that prepared the study, including Richard Bissell, "who officially entered the CIA as special assistant to CIA Director Dulles shortly thereafter and helped plan the Guatemalan operation."[58] The report was prepared to win congressional and public support for the U.S. overthrow of Arbenz. As a followup, the NPA published a report defending the actions of United Fruit in Guatemala against its critics.[59]

After the Eisenhower administration successfully aided the overthrow of the Arbenz government, investors and would-be investors pressured the administration to establish the institutional channels for an expansion of aid to Guatemala. The expansion of aid to Guatemala was a precursor to the expanded aid programs for Latin America during the Alliance for Progress and the Central American Common Market, (chap. 4).

The Shift to "Trade and Aid" in Guatemala

Having convinced domestic industrialists within their own party of the urgency of responding to the Communist threat, internationalists succeeded in substantially increasing the level of U.S. aid to the country. Between 1954 and 1958, U.S. aid to Guatemala soared to $90 million, compared with just $60 million and $61 million in U.S. aid to all of Latin America in fiscal years 1956 and 1957, respectively.[60] U.S. investors and would-be investors were the primary beneficiaries of U.S. government lending programs for Guatemala.

The Eisenhower administration sought to promote Guatemala as a showcase for foreign direct investment and as an inducement to other Latin American countries to follow the developmental path conducive to further U.S. investment. Unable to rely on "trade not aid" in its efforts to expand U.S. direct investments in Guatemala, the Eisenhower administration shifted to a "trade and aid" strategy pushed emphatically by internationalists after 1954.

The "trade and aid" strategy toward Guatemala included efforts by the Eisenhower administration to create the preconditions for further U.S. investment there. First, the administration worked with a private U.S. consulting firm, Klein and Saks, and the U.S.-backed government of Castillo Armas to remove obstacles to foreign direct investment that had been established by Arbenz. The Armas government repealed lawsuits pending against IRCA and Empressa Electrica, returned land to United Fruit, and signed a "new contract favorable to the company."[61] The government then repealed legislation that taxed profits remitted abroad, and it "became the third Latin American government to sign an Investment Guarantee Agreement with the U.S. government, under which U.S. enterprises were insured against losses from currency inconvertibility and expropriation."[62]

Finally, the Eisenhower administration paid Klein and Saks to work with the Guatemalan government to devise a five-year economic plan designed to encourage foreign direct investment. The plan established a tax code favorable to U.S. companies, including provisions for the development of massive infrastructure projects (roads, communications and power networks) to be built by U.S. firms. As Susanne Jonas put it, the Eisenhower administration developed an aid apparatus for Guatemala that relied on a "parallel government" of U.S. administrators and private consultants to dramatically expand programs beneficial to private industry.[63]

Immediately after the 1954 coup, the Eisenhower administration authorized a grant to Guatemala totaling $6,425,000. Of that amount, $1,425,000 was for cooperative construction of the Inter-American Highway, $1,300,000 was for technical assistance, and $3,200,000 was grant aid for "unspecified economic development projects," most of which went to U.S. construction firms such as Johnson-Drake and Piper for improvement and extension of the South Coastal Highway.[64]

In addition, the oil companies Union, Richmond, Jersey Standard, and Atlantic pressured the Eisenhower administration to finance the services of U.S. private consultant Elmer Batzell to draft a new petroleum law and corresponding regulations for the Guatemalan government. A communiqué from the U.S. embassy to the State Department strongly urged the administration to pick up the tab for Batzell, warning that "unless Batzell is retained the field will be left to Venezuelan advisers, whose work will not produce a law acceptable to U.S. companies."[65] Susanne Jonas summarizes the new Petroleum Code:

The Code . . . provided for the cession of subsoil rights to foreign oil companies, and even permitted them to maintain their concessions as unused reserves, for up to 40 years. The companies would enjoy tax rates lower than in the United States, and a 27.5 % depletion allowance . . . Several dozen U.S. oil companies rushed in to take advantage of this giveaway measure. Within a year after passage of the Code, U.S. companies had solicited concessions totaling more than half the area of Guatemala. By February 1957, the U.S. business press reported that "major oil companies have occupied most of the office space available and have leased many of the new houses for their officials."[66]

In addition to providing the infrastructure, tax codes, and investment incentives for increased foreign direct investment, the Eisenhower administration pursued a strategy for light industry in Guatemala that was similar to the Point Four program in El Salvador (see chap. 2). Through its technical assistance program, the administration promoted the construction of power, roads, and communications facilities necessary for the influx of light-manufacturing industry in the country. The strategy was to expand industrial production by relying on the purchasing power of the Central American upper and middle classes.

Such an approach diverged from the nationalistic efforts of Arbenz, who had sought to industrialize by expanding the domestic market through land reform and mild redistribution of wealth. In contrast, the Eisenhower administration supported an industrialization scheme that would avoid the "destabilizing" effects of expansion in the domestic market, relying instead on the potential buying power of an enlarged regional market.

Initially, the administration hoped that the goal could be accomplished through existing bilateral treaties that would lower the transaction costs of trade among the Central American countries.[67] The failure of the Guatemalan experiment to attract a sufficient level of foreign direct investment convinced the administration and private

U.S. investors that future U.S. aid packages should be expanded to encompass plans for a Central American Common Market.

The Lessons of Guatemala: The Need for Trade and Aid

By 1958, private business interests close to the Eisenhower administration saw a move toward a Central American Common Market as necessary for a number of reasons. First, efforts to significantly expand foreign direct investment in manufacturing in Central America had lagged behind the expectations of leading U.S. investors. Leading investors and would-be investors in Central America, including Rockefeller's Basic Economy Corporation, the Grace Corporation, Pillsbury, Alcoa, Lenox, Phelps Dodge, Esso, and leading U.S. banks such as Chase Manhattan and First National City Bank, were frustrated by the limited opportunities of the existing bilateral treaties for encouraging foreign investment. The treaties had failed to lower significantly the trade barriers among Central American countries.

Second, leading investors were convinced that only an expanded regional market under U.S. government direction could support an expansion of foreign direct investment in manufacturing. In short, the "trade and aid" strategy toward Guatemala needed to be expanded to include the entire Central American region.[68] Under such a scheme, the U.S. government would expand aid to the region in the form of money for a regional development bank, and private consortiums would channel funds toward investments within a common market internally free of tariff barriers.

Third, business internationalists began to see the development of such a common market as the only viable option for the promotion of direct foreign investment in the region. Nationalists within the Republican party continued to block efforts by internationalists to liberalize trade. Tariffs on a whole series of light manufactured goods, including textiles and chemicals, remained in place by 1958, frustrating the efforts of internationalists within the CED, CFR, and NPA who wanted to pursue a strategy of export-led industrialization in the Third World. David Baldwin has described how the protectionist bloc in Congress opposed efforts of the Eisenhower administration to liberalize trade:

Congressional behavior in the 1958-1962 period gave the free traders little cause to rejoice. In 1958 President Eisenhower was able to secure renewal of the Reciprocal Trade Agreements Act for four years in the midst of a situation which prompted one student of American foreign policy to note: "Seldom has there been such a strong and well-organized protest against the admission into the American market of foreign-made goods." Despite President Eisenhower's success in extending the life of the Reciprocal Trade Agreements Program, Congress inserted into the act for the first time a provision for legislative veto of tariff decisions by the President.[69]

Throughout the 1950s, internationalists of the Republican party dominated in the executive branch and nationalist Republicans exerted considerable influence in Congress. Internationalists within the CFR, CED, and NPA had long recognized import-substituting industrialization as a possible strategy in promoting increased direct foreign investment in manufacturing in the Third World.[70] Until 1958, however, most internationalists still hoped to pursue trade liberalization at home that would facilitate the preferential option of export-led industrialization in Central America. That hope was foiled when nationalists proved able to maintain tariff barriers on a variety of manufactured products that U.S. investors and would-be investors hoped to produce in Central America, including textiles, processed foods, and chemicals.[71]

Both nationalists and internationalists were concerned about the rise of Soviet influence in Latin America during the late 1950s. Internationalists justified increased aid to Central America, including aid for the Central American Common Market, on national security grounds.

Given the nationalist strength in Congress, internationalists pressured the Eisenhower administration in 1958 to pursue a Central American Common Market suitable to U.S. investors. As we will see in the next chapter, such pressure helped convince the administration to schedule a meeting with Salvadoran president José Maria Lemus to discuss the initial plans for the formation of the Central American Common Market.

Some internationalists, frustrated by the slow response of the Eisenhower administration to their concerns, began to rely on the Democratic party by the late 1950s and early 1960s. Chapter 4 examines business and government support for the creation and operation of the CACM and the relative influence of business groups on the Eisenhower and Kennedy administrations.

4

Business Welcomes Creation of Central American Common Market

Internationalists expressed support for regional common markets in the 1958 Rockefeller Panel Reports, written and endorsed by corporate internationalists of the Council on Foreign Relations and the National Planning Association.[1] The panel reports were made available to the Eisenhower administration prior to a March 1958 meeting between President Eisenhower and Salvadoran President José Maria Lemus. In a memo from administration official C. Edward Galbreath to Clarence Randall, a close adviser on Latin American affairs, Galbreath refers favorably to the main recommendations of the Rockefeller Reports, which include "support for regional common markets and international commmodity price stabilization schemes."[2]

In the reports, internationalists led by Rockefeller's International Basic Economy Corporation, with increased investment stakes in El Salvador and elsewhere in Central and South America, articulated their preference for U.S. government support for a Central American Common Market. As the reports indicated, the primary reasons for the support were economic, not anticommunist. The Rockefeller Panel began its endorsement of the CACM with the following general observations about Latin America: "At present the intertrade among the Latin American nations amounts to less than 10 percent of their total trade. This compares with a figure of about 50 per cent for Western Europe's intertrade. Historically, most Latin American economies have been oriented toward overseas trade with Europe or the United States. Trade within the area has been hampered by a lack of transportation and by tariffs, quotas, and inconvertible currencies."[3]

The reports went on to argue that there was an urgent need to expand opportunities for investment and trade within a regional common market.

> The Latin American economy . . . has now reached a stage of development in which greater freedom of trade within the area would contribute to general growth. Industrialization in many nations is now outrunning local makets. Yet the barriers to trade are such that few industries in Latin America can serve more than a protected local market. In short, industry is bursting at the seams, and it would be logical to widen the scope of industrial activity by removing present constraints. Any steps that Latin American countries take toward eliminating internal barriers and working toward broader regional development planning in harmony with the general economic growth of the free world deserve our support.[4]

The reports argued that a primary aim of the U.S. government should be "to encourage private overseas investment as a complement to programs of economic aid and technical assistance."[5] If foreign investors were to be attracted, the panel cited an urgent need to improve the investment climate, since "private investment . . . will flow into foreign fields only if there is the prospect of a return commensurate with the risks involved."[6]

The reports specified several ways to improve the investment climate in Latin America. The first was the promotion of regional common markets that permit "men, money, and goods to move freely to where they can play the most important role in world economic growth."[7] Second, the panel urged the U.S. government to encourage the "coordination of private and public activities" to help promote the necessary preconditions for increased foreign direct investment.[8] This step would require more detailed information about the projects of U.S. companies so as to facilitate the development of an infrastructure appropriate for industrial expansion.

The panel listed as an example the forest reserve of Honduras, where U.S. companies were interested in developing a "paper and pulp industry capable of supplying a large part of Latin America."[9] The role of U.S. aid agencies would be to facilitate this private effort with public projects such as road building, which would help "eliminate bottlenecks [that] prevent further expansion."[10] The panel also urged the EXIM Bank to make its intergovernmental loans "less time consuming and more productive" by developing "appropriate combinations of private and public capital."[11]

As a third recommendation, the panel urged the U.S. government to "introduce the managerial and technical skills of private in-

vestment into areas where the normal standards for private investment decision would not induce such investment." [12] As a means to
this end, the panel recommended the extension of "long-term, low
interest rate loans to private enterprise as a special inducement to go
into such areas." [13]

The reports identified the newly created Development Loan
Fund as a likely vehicle for such an effort. When other methods
failed to induce private investment abroad, the "Development Loan
Fund should be given the authority to contract with American private enterprises to render certain services of a technical or managerial character," rather than "making an outright grant to state-
operated oranizations." [14] The panel also indicated that "regional development authorities" (such as the Central American Bank for Economic Development, created alongside the Central American Common Market) could help promote investment by providing loans for
infrastructure and investment projects. [15]

Finally, the panel called for the formation of an Inter-American
Payments Union with capital contributions from all nations of the
Western Hemisphere. Such a facility would provide credit to member
countries to "cushion the adjustments entailed by shifts in the international economy." [16] The Payments Union was seen as an "essential
first step in broadening markets throughout the area" by making it
possible for nations to "maintain their imports of materials, machinery, and equipment needed for economic development." [17] The facility would be needed to break down currency restrictions and regulations that can "impede trade as effectively as tariffs and quotas." [18]
The panel insisted that such a union "would provide a tremendous
impetus to economic development by making it possible for industries to serve the entire area, instead of individual nations." [19] As
such, the creation of a Payments Union was seen as proceeding
"hand in hand with steps to set up either a general or regional common market." [20]

The Rockefeller Reports represented the most concise and detailed
expression of business support for U.S. assistance to the CACM. However, as early as 1953, the National Foreign Trade Council (NFTC) had
supported the integration movement sponsored by the Economic
Commission for Latin America. The NFTC believed that Central American integration would "spur forward economic growth and further
possibilities of United States investment." [21] Following the NFTC report, the Department of Commerce in 1956 indicated that U.S. busi-

nesses were interested in a regional market in Central America as a means to enhance investment options. The report noted the following:

A factor of considerable interest to the potential investor in Central America is the trend in recent years toward a closer economic relationship among the Central American Republics. Obviously if the boundaries that divide the five Central American countries were to be eliminated and the whole area were to form a single free market with more than nine million people, investment opportunities would be far more numerous. Many industries find too great a risk involved in becoming established in a country having 1, 2, or 3 million people whose standard of living is relatively low.[22]

The report concluded that Central American integration would not conflict with U.S. trade policies: "The gradual creation of a free-trade area in Central America would be consistent with United States as well as GATT (General Agreement on Tariffs and Trade) policies. Despite the fact that the Central American countries, through these treaties, grant exclusive privilege to each other, this departure from the most-favored-nation rule has been generally accepted because of the geographical propinquity and historical ties among the Central American countries and because of the proclaimed goal of a customs union."[23]

By 1958, a number of investors were interested in promoting or expanding projects in Central America. These internationalists, in regular contacts with the State Department, indicated their support for a Central American Common Market. The firms included General Tire and Rubber, which had a plant in Guatemala and was looking to expand to another location; Dillon, Read, and Company, which had secured an $8 million investment in a fertilizer plant in El Salvador; and Crown Zellerbach Corp. and National Bulk Carriers, which were interested in a $30 million paper and pulp mill in Honduras, an investment referred to by the business sponsors of the Rockefeller Report as in need of public assistance to make it profitable.[24] In addition, the *Wall Street Journal* noted the general support from international investors for U.S. government efforts to develop the Central American Common Market as "a step toward greater stability"—a step that had investors gambling that "the plan won't collapse along the way."[25]

In addition to corporate support for the Common Market, there is evidence of direct business involvement with the U.S. government in the initial steps to promote a CACM favorable to U.S. investors. The

Eisenhower administration made public its support for the CACM at
the March 1958 meeting with Salavadoran President Lemus. The administration heralded a pilot project between El Salvador and Honduras as an initial step on the road to economic integration, "which
seemed a more practical approach than waiting for all of the countries
to agree on a method [for integration]."[26]

The U.S. government enlisted the support of leading internationalists. On March 16, 1959, John J. McCloy, chairman of the board
of the Chase Manhattan Bank, and Thomas J. Pettyman, chairman of
the board of the National Coffee Association, organized a luncheon
that brought Lemus together with U.S. investors interested in the
opportunities of a CACM.[27] Pettyman was close to a number of U.S.
industrialists interested in pursuing investments in food processing
in the region.

U.S. business interests worked actively with the State Department and the Agency for International Development on expanding
public assistance to institutions designed to facilitate the growth of a
CACM favorable to U.S. business interests. By the late 1950s, the
Eisenhower administration had begun its move from "trade not aid"
to "trade and aid" in Central America, with the intention of fostering
a more favorable environment for U.S. investors.

The Administration Shifts Its Stance

The administration's shift to a "trade and aid" policy originated from
three main concerns expressed by business internationalists and administration officials. The first was the realization that some Latin
American economies, particularly in Central America, lacked the infrastructure necessary for increased private investment. The administration believed that public lending had to be stepped up to encourage the development of viable free market economies. A spring 1957
report of the U.S. Council on Foreign Economic Policy summarized
this view:

The real hope for development in this area lies in the growth of private enterprise, both domestic and foreign. In several countries in the area private enterprise can presently look forward to fewer obstacles to investment in the
future. In other countries, however, the lack of resources and the failure to
understand the advantages of private investment may deter real growth. The
lack of capital resources is reflected in the inadequate roads and other transportation facilities and in poor health and sanitary conditions. Aside from

private development capital in agriculture and certain extractive industries, the lack of basic public facilities is a deterrent to private investment.[28]

The report went on to note the need for a shift in foreign economic policy toward the region:

It would be prudent to take another look at the need for low-interest, long-term capital loans to the area, and to measure United States interests there as opposed to other areas of the world where such loans are made. The present policy of no develop mental loans except in emergency conditions is not consistent with the need for such capital and United States interests in the area. Ultimately, the development of the area depends upon the effective encouragement of private investment. There are some conditions, however, which must be improved before private investment can be achieved.[29]

A second major concern of U.S. policy makers was the decline in world prices for the narrow range of basic commodities exported from Latin America. Business internationalists close to the administration worried that such trends would make it increasingly difficult for U.S. firms to take advantage of investment opportunities within the region. Exporters were concerned that Latin American countries would be unable to afford U.S. goods.[30]

The terms of trade of Central American countries faced a sharp decline in 1958 when compared with 1954, as reflected in falling coffee and banana prices on the world market. The trend, exacerbated by price inelasticity in the United States for such commodities, generated concern among business internationalists in communication with the Eisenhower administration. The administration noted the urgency of the economic problems in a classified National Security Council document of November 26, 1958. It cited the falling commodity prices as a "major problem" in U.S.-Latin American relations, and it characterized Latin American governments as "slow to take the necessary economic measures to deal with these problems."[31]

A third concern of the administration was the inability to check the influence of economic nationalists within the United States, who continued to maintain trade restrictions on textiles, chemicals, lead, and zinc. The restrictions made it difficult to pursue a strategy of export-led growth in Latin America. Business internationalists close to the administration began to advocate U.S. economic and political assistance for import-substituting industrialization behind a regional common market.

Internationalists saw such a strategy as promoting trade and investment options within an enlarged regional market, thereby eclipsing the limitations on foreign investment posed by existing bilateral treaties. In addition, a U.S.-directed regional market promised to break down most or all barriers to the free flow of goods within Central America. Trade had been inhibited during the 1950s by the existence of limited bilateral treaties between Central American countries. As we will see, the Eisenhower and Kennedy administrations sought to extend aid to regional economic and political institutions that could enhance the prospects of increased foreign investment behind regional tariff barriers.

Both administrations were aware that such a program would undoubtedly bring with it significant political changes within the region. Any effort to promote ISI inevitably meant a growth of urban populations and the increased potential for labor organizing in the region. ISI might also disrupt peasant life, as farm workers and landless peasants moved to the cities to find work.

The Eisenhower and Kennedy administrations sought the support of U.S. business and labor in checking the development of radical unions in rural and urban areas. The best example was the American Institute for Free Labor Development (AIFLD), a cooperative government-business-labor venture created to offer moderate alternatives to labor strikes and mass mobilizations in the region. The venture was not a defensive response to the threat of communism but a safeguard against the radicalizing effects of U.S. promotion of ISI strategies.

The next sections of this chapter highlight the specific measures undertaken by Eisenhower and Kennedy to pursue a "trade and aid" strategy for Latin America. By 1958, the Eisenhower administration had reversed itself and had thrown its weight behind ISI, a price stabilization scheme, and an Inter-American Development Bank. The shift toward soft loans and support for ISI was seen as essential to promote a regional common market, deemed necessary for increased foreign investment and economic development. For the Eisenhower and Kennedy administrations, increased foreign investment and economic development were largely synonymous. Business internationalists close to both administrations left their mark on aid programs to Central America throughout the 1960s.

U.S. Influence on the Inter-American Development Bank

In moving to support a program of expanded aid to Central America, the State Department focused on building regional lending institutions that could promote the integration of the Central American economies. The most important of these were the Inter-American Development Bank (IDB) and the Central American Bank for Economic Integration (CABEI).

The efforts of the Eisenhower administration to promote multilateral lending for the CACM reflected the influence of business internationalists—U.S. investors represented by the CFR, the CED, the NPA, and the NFTC. The administration agreed that the economic development of Central America hinged on its ability to attract foreign investors. With this objective in mind, U.S. policy makers sought to influence the direction of Central American integration.

One way U.S. policy makers exerted influence over Latin American states was through regional organizations. As early as 1948, the Truman administration had encouraged the creation of the Organization of American States (OAS) "to provide facilities for United States investors wishing to exploit the resources of Latin America."[32] The United States had signaled its political influence over the OAS in 1954 with the passage of a resolution that updated the Monroe Doctrine and was targeted especially toward the justification of U.S. intervention in Guatemala. In the resolution, the U.S. announced its "authority" to intervene in the hemisphere in order to check the "domination or control of the political institutions of any American state by the international communist movement."[33]

In 1958, U.S. policy makers used their influence with the Inter-American Economic and Social Council of the OAS to advance the creation of the Inter-American Development Bank, which would promote the preconditions for foreign direct investment in Latin America. Latin American officials had long advocated such an institution as a means of access to development loans. In 1958, U.S. officials supported the IDB on the condition that it be used to enhance the opportunities of private investors, both local and foreign, through the promotion of regional integration.

Given its predominant economic and political clout, the United States was instrumental in shaping both the initial proposals for an IDB and the eventual structure and orientation of the multilateral bank. In fact, the creation of the IDB was contingent on U.S. financial and political support. In a 1958 document prepared by the general secretariat of the OAS with the advice and cooperation of U.S. and Latin American officials, the OAS advocated the creation of an IDB that would facilitate private foreign investment. The OAS report emphasized the obstacles to economic development faced by Latin American states that lacked access to development funding in the form of currently available bilateral and multilateral loans.

The report emphasized the inadequacy of EXIM and the World Bank for furthering the development needs of Latin America. OAS officials argued that an IDB was needed to provide soft loans for infrastructure and technical assistance that would support increased local and foreign private investment. The report insisted that "the promotion of private foreign investment, both within Latin America and outside, should be a major responsibility and concern of a regional development institution."[34] The IDB was to pursue the following objectives in promoting foreign investment:

1. Assisting member governments in developing programs for attracting foreign private investment.
2. Providing a clearinghouse for information on investment opportunities in Latin American countries.
3. Assisting foreign investors in finding local financing for investments in Latin America.
4. Promoting joint ventures involving both local and foreign capital and enterprise.
5. Making loans to foreign investors, including Latin American enterprises whose activities would promote regional integration.
6. Organizing conferences of local and foreign businessmen and Latin American government officials to explore problems relating to private investment in Latin America.[35]

The Eisenhower administration used its political and economic influence in the OAS to promote the creation of an IDB that would facilitate U.S. interests. A major objective was to direct the lending programs of the IDB toward the promotion of infrastructure needed to achieve regional integration. At times, the U.S. government worked with business internationalists to devise lending programs that would greatly accelerate the level of foreign direct investment in the region. These multilateral programs complemented the efforts of the Eisenhower and Kennedy administrations to expand bilateral assistance to the regional integration effort. In shifting to a policy of "trade and aid," both administrations attempted to lower the costs of production for U.S. direct investors and to promote the creation of viable market economies that could check nationalist and Soviet political challenges to U.S. interests.

U.S. policy makers used their financial and political clout to promote multilateral lending favorable to U.S. investors. The U.S. monetary contribution to the IDB has given the U.S. representative approximately 40 percent of the total votes concerning the allocation of loans. During the creation of the IDB, the Eisenhower administration insisted that any allocation of concessionary funds be subject to a two-thirds vote, which gave the United States veto power over soft loan monies from the bank.[36] As a result, the U.S. representative to the IDB was able to exercise considerable influence over the criteria used to allocate funds.

The National Advisory Council, composed of the secretary of the treasury (acting chairman), the secretary of state, the secretary of commerce, the chairman of the board of governors of the federal reserve system, and the chairman and president of the Export-Import Bank, has established the criteria that determine whether or not the U.S. executive director of the IDB will vote yes or no on a particular loan. As noted by Peter DeWitt in his extensive study of the IDB, the criteria "are the result of U.S. congressional legislation and executive orders designed to persuade loan-requesting countries to adopt policies in accord with the U.S. national interest."[37] Through regulations established via executive order and through legislation, the NAC requires that the U.S. representative to the IDB vote against any loan to countries that have: 1. Expropriated, nationalized, or seized ownership of U.S. property. 2. Taken steps to repudiate or nullify existing contracts or agreements with U.S. representatives. 3. Imposed or enforced discriminatory taxes or other assessments against any U.S. citizen, corporation, or association not less than 50 percent of which is owned by U.S. citizens.[38]

U.S. officials were instrumental in promoting regional integration projects as the cornerstone of IDB loans. The U.S. representative to the IDB pursued the interests of the Eisenhower and Kennedy administrations in utilizing the multilateral bank to further the economic integration of Central America. At its founding, the IDB institutionalized its commitment to regional integration as part of the "Establishing Agreement for the Bank," which identified the IDB as the "Bank of Integration."[39] As Peter DeWitt notes, since 1959 the bank has promoted regional projects that further the objective of economic integration:

The Bank management has institutionalized the integration strategy within the IDB's organizational structure and has adopted a number of integrationist policies, which exert external constraints on its activities in Latin America. One such decision was the establishment in 1965 of the Office of Integration Advisor, which links the Bank more directly with other integration agencies.

Through this office the Bank endeavors to devise formulas at the regional and national level to support regional economic integration as the basic instrument of social and economic development in Latin America.[40]

Under the integration strategy it pursues, the IDB promotes direct foreign investment through loans for infrastructure, technical assistance, and capital goods. The IDB has given priority to infrastructural loans since its founding, with the majority of financing devoted to the development of transportation and electric power necessary for profitable foreign investment.

The IDB has worked with the U.S. government and multinational corporations in the development and implementation of its lending programs. The best example is the effort of the multilateral bank to extend loans to projects undertaken by the Atlantic Community Group for the Development of Latin America (ADELA), a multinational investment company that relies on fifty-four of the largest U.S. corporations for 50 percent of its capital subscriptions.[41] In its annual investment report of 1968, ADELA summarized its "close" relationship with IDB:

In addition to the $10 million long term loan granted by IDB to ADELA for financing small and medium range projects which are not within IDB's direct reach, IDB has made parallel loans to larger projects in which we have invested. With the IFC [International Finance Corporation of the World Bank] we have an increasing number of joint projects including joint sponsorship of very large investments. With both institutions there exists a continuous contact and free exchange of information so as to avoid duplication of effort in the areas of development and evaluating investment opportunities.[42]

The Eisenhower administration's shift to "trade and aid" did not stop with the IDB. The Eisenhower and Kennedy administrations also influenced the operating structure and lending priorities of the Central American Bank for Economic Integration (CABEI). The Kennedy administration expanded U.S. bilateral aid to the region via the Agency for International Development in 1961, as well as creating the Regional Office for Central America and Panama (ROCAP), which supervised the allocation of technical advice and monetary assistance to the Central American integration effort, including the CABEI.

This complex structure of U.S. support for the regional integration effort ensured that bilateral and multilateral financing of development projects would be designed to facilitate the expansion of infrastructure and capital necessary for increased foreign direct investment. In fact, as in the case of the IDB, business internationalists worked with the

State Department through AID to design and implement programs attractive to U.S. investors.

U.S. Influence on the Development Policies of the Central American Bank for Economic Integration

In 1959 the Eisenhower administration sent two State Department representatives on a fact-finding mission to Central America to push for the creation of the CACM. The U.S. reps met with Salvadoran officials to discuss the prospects of creating a regional common market characterized by "low external tariffs and complete freedom of movement of goods, capital and people" within three years.[43] Promising to channel $100 million through two funds to help finance the integration process, U.S. policy makers convinced the governments of El Salvador, Honduras, and Guatemala to sign the Tripartite Agreement of Economic Association in February 1960. It provided for "immediate free trade for almost all commodities originating in member nations, and, in principle, [for] the free movement of capital and people."[44]

Through this 1960 treaty, which Nicaragua joined in 1961 and Costa Rica in 1963, U.S. officials institutionalized their influence over the direction and pace of the integration movement. The terms of the 1960 treaty bypassed ECLA's slower-paced moves toward integration. ECLA's 1958 treaty represented an effort to limit the number of products eligible for free trade and to move gradually toward complete free trade over a period of 10 years.[45]

The State Department bypassed ECLA's proposals for gradual integration through its influence over the policies of the Central American Bank for Economic Integration. U.S. policy makers used the Agency for International Development to restrict CABEI loans to projects endorsed by U.S. officials. AID's task force report of 1961 pushed for the creation of the Regional Office of Central America and Panama (ROCAP) to establish the institutional channels to further U.S. objectives. The objectives included "improving private investment" in Central America, making sure that "integration did not take a direction detrimental to U.S. interests," coordinating "U.S. policies and programs for Central American integration agencies," and channeling "U.S. technical and financial assistance."[46]

Since its founding in 1961, the CABEI has depended on ROCAP and the Inter-American Development Bank for most of its resources. A study completed in April 1969 revealed that: "the Bank's overall resources amounted to $250 million, of which $215 million (or 86 percent) came from foreign sources—about three-fourths from the United States and the Inter-American Development Bank, where the United States has decisive influence, and the other fourth from suppliers' credits granted by some Western European countries and Mexico.[47]

AID, through its regional office in Guatemala, has used its lending power to influence the policies of the CABEI. AID's first $5 million loan was accompanied by a requirement (clause 6.09 of basic loan agreement) that AID give prior approval of further borrowing by CABEI and that further disbursements on the initial loan could be suspended if AID disapproved of debts incurred by the Bank.[48] Through extensive political pressure by AID officials, the Central American Board of Governors eventually agreed to the terms of the first loan. ROCAP, an AID affiliate, has also worked to ensure that CABEI adheres to certain conditions in order to be eligible for AID money. The conditions established in 1962 included (1) tying of aid to goods and services purchased in the U.S.; (2) shipping goods on U.S. flag vessels; (3) U.S. approval of all subcontracts; and 4) no trade with socialist countries.[49]

U.S. policy makers also used AID to weaken the "integration industries" treaty signed by the five Central American countries in 1958. The integration treaty sought to protect certain Central American firms from competition by granting them exclusive free trade privileges for the regional market as designated "integration industries." This protection evolved from ECLA's conclusion that only one plant in specified product lines could be sustained by the Common Market. The integration plan was also designed to promote balanced development by preventing the concentration of industries within one or two countries. The integration industry plan stipulated that each country have at least one integration industry before any country could receive a second one.

U.S. policy makers opposed the integration scheme as contrary to the U.S. interest in promoting free trade throughout the region. In their statements opposing integration industries, U.S. officials cited the negative impact of such industries on U.S. business interests. A State Department document explained the problems with integration industries in the following terms: "Many private investors . . . have hesitated to invest in Central America because they fear possible discrimination under the Regime. No investor can ever be sure that designation of an industry related to his . . . will not seriously affect his

own business. . . . The effect [of these problems] on potential investment from abroad is serious."[50]

U.S. policy makers were concerned that integration industries
would limit the opportunities for U.S. investors in the region. In a
March 1962 meeting, a U.S. official helping to direct U.S. policy toward regional integration implied that U.S. companies were holding
back investments in Central America because the integration plan
"excludes the possibility of competition by other U.S. firms, and this
naturally is not well-received in the U.S."[51] As a result, U.S. officials
attempted to weaken the integration industries scheme in several
ways:

1.) A stipulation in the General Treaty of Integration that granted immediate free trade to nearly all products in the region.
2.) The U.S. refusal to allow AID funds channeled through CABEI to be
used for subloans to regional integration industries.
3.) The U.S. prevention of other lending institutions, especially the IDB,
from making loans to integration industries.
4.) The U.S. pressure on CABEI not to finance integration industries
from other funds.[52]

U.S. policy makers used their political and economic influence
with the CABEI to institutionalize aid policies favorable to U.S. investors. During the 1960s, the CABEI granted a considerable portion of
its loans to U.S. investors, along with guarantees to foreign investors
of no discrimination in lending policies, free access to the regional
market, rights to take over local industries, and rights to import technology.[53] By 1970, CABEI had extended 32 percent of its loans to
foreign-controlled firms, and "an additional 34 percent to regionally
controlled firms with foreign equity or technical assistance partners."[54] The CABEI has channeled most of its loans to infrastructure
and private industry, a practice consistent with the goals of U.S. policy makers in pursuing a "trade and aid" strategy toward Central
America.

A Dramatic Increase in Bilateral Assistance to Latin America

This study has thus far emphasized the continuity between the Eisenhower and Kennedy administrations in the shift to a "trade and aid"
foreign economic policy. As early as 1958, the Eisenhower administration moved to exert its political and economic influence over multilateral development banks involved in Central American economic in-

tegration. Without the financial support of the United States, the move toward Central American integration likely would have stalled.

The continuity in Eisenhower's 1958 foreign economic policies and the policies of his successors, however, should not obscure the significant differences—in particular, the Kennedy administration's dramatic increase in bilateral assistance to Latin America through the Alliance for Progress. The Eisenhower administration's move toward "trade and aid" was largely reflected in financial and political support for multilateral development banks and the shift toward soft lending. The dramatic expansion of bilateral assistance for Latin America did not occur until the Kennedy administration unleashed its Alliance for Progress in 1961.

Kennedy officials greatly expanded bilateral lending programs in 1961 with the creation of the Agency for International Development (AID), which combined and extended the programs of the Development Loan Fund and the International Cooperation Administration. As we will see in this section, the institutionalization of "trade and aid" was completed by State Department and congressional authorization for expanded bilateral assistance to Latin America during the Kennedy administration.

Bilateral assistance programs for Central America increased dramatically during the Kennedy and Johnson years (table 1), with the notable exception of aid to Guatemala, which had been receiving increased assistance since the 1950s (see chap. 3).

What accounts for the expansion of bilateral assistance under these Democratic administrations? Most explanations focus on the impact of international politics, such as the growing Soviet threat and the rise of the Castro regime in Cuba. These explanations are part of the reason for the shift to "trade and aid." But what is as significant, I believe, is the policy recommendations of diverse business sectors close to the Eisenhower and Kennedy administrations.

The recommendations of business elites reveal that there was no monolithic response to the communist threat. Instead, business internationalists advocated a shift in foreign economic policy that reflected their sectoral position in the world economy and that differed considerably from the policy recommendations of economic nationalists. The fact that the Republican party was divided between internationalists and nationalists as part of its foreign policy constituency tells us more about Republicans' hesitancy in shifting toward a "trade and aid" foreign economic policy than does the "communist threat."

During the Eisenhower administration, the business elites of the

Table 1.   U.S. Aid to Central America, 1957-71
(In Millions of Dollars)

Country	1957-61	1962-66	1967-71
Costa Rica	$17.64	$57.00	$72.7
El Salvador	8.70	78.80	44.1
Guatemala	64.10	54.50	89.6
Honduras	23.70	46.60	43.2
Nicaragua	14.60	68.30	56.5

Source: U.S. AID, U.S. Overseas Loans & Grants & Assistance from International Organizations, July 1, 1945-June 30, 1971 (Washington, D.C.: GPO, May 24, 1972).

Republican party were significantly divided along economic and ideological lines. This schism was reflected in the coexistence of diverse business interest groups that battled for influence over the direction of foreign economic policy. As we have seen in previous chapters, business internationalists represented by the CFR, the CED, the NPA, and the liberal Rockefeller wing of the party represented the "progressive" voice, advocating a "trade and aid" foreign economic policy. These groups were less concerned with the "Soviet threat" than they were with investment opportunities in Latin America and nationalist threats to those investments. These internationalists had considerable investments abroad, relative to other business interests, and they spoke of a need to increase aid programs dramatically to pave the way for increased foreign investments, such as infrastructure, subsidies, and technical assistance, which many Third World countries lacked.

Business internationalists were close to the Eisenhower State Department. State Department officials endorsed the Rockefeller Report of 1958, which represented the most extensive elaboration of a "trade and aid" strategy by business internationalists of the CFR and the NPA.[55] Other business internationalists with the Business Advisory Council (BAC) and the CED were well represented in the Eisenhower administration: Eisenhower himself was a long-time member of the CED, and prominent officeholders in the State Department and Commerce belonged to each of these business groups.[56]

At the same time, the Republican party depended upon business nationalists within the National Association of Manufacturers and the chambers of commerce for substantial monetary and political support. While Fortune 500 companies dominated the internationalist organizations, the NAM and the Chambers of Commerce during the 1950s were dominated by small and medium-sized businesses that could not afford to invest abroad and that remained vulnerable to imports.

These groups have been referred to as fundamentalists because of their right-wing (sometimes far-right) political views on foreign and domestic policy. Their tenuous economic position and their relative dependence on labor for a high percentage of value added in production have given these companies an economic stake in low social spending and protectionist foreign economic policies.[57]

These interest groups were especially influential within the Republican party, both through Congress and through the Treasury Department via such allies as George Humphrey, who as secretary of the treasury from 1953 to 1957 argued against increases in foreign aid (see chap. 2). The influence of the fundamentalists within the Republican party helps explain why the Eisenhower administration was reluctant and in fact unable to pursue fully a "trade and aid" strategy. As David Baldwin has noted, these business elites helped block increases in foreign lending from 1958 through 1962.[58]

The influence of business nationalists on the Republican party is also illustrated by their dominance of the party by the early 1960s. As Ferguson and Rogers have noted:

The always tenuous position of the liberal Republicans within the GOP was disintegrating completely. With the growing boom, imports exploded, threatening many traditional, labor-intensive Republican manufacturers, as well as some primary producers and national oil concerns. Joined by many agricultural interests and smaller businesses who received little or no benefit from the investment-oriented tax cuts and who often feared the effects of rising social spending on their supplies of low-wage, unskilled labor; copper companies, whose prices were collapsing; some defense contractors; and many leftover opponents of the New Deal—these groups went on the offensive. Though at the time they represented a minority of Americans, they constituted a majority of Republicans. After a series of bitter primaries, this coalition seized complete control of the party. Party elites wrote an import-restriction clause right into the party platform. They also denounced the U.N., internationalism, and (memorably) the Rockefellers, as they nominated Barry Goldwater for President.[59]

The impact of business nationalists on the Republican party is significant in understanding the different approaches taken by the Eisenhower and Kennedy administrations in foreign economic policy. The Eisenhower administration spent much of its energy trying to placate both wings of the Republican party. Business nationalists represented by the NAM and the Chamber of Commerce fought against most measures to increase foreign economic assistance. The recommendations of the Hoover Commission of 1955 represented the views of business nationalists close to the Republican party. The report called for slowing the rate of foreign economic assistance at the same time that internationalists within the party were arguing for a shift to "trade and aid."[60]

By 1960 many leading internationalists prominent in drafting the Rockefeller Report of 1958 shifted their allegiance to the Kennedy administration. In fact, the business leaders of the National Planning Association and the Council on Foreign Relations played a leading role in drafting the ambitious foreign lending programs of the Alliance for Progress, which completed the institutionalization of a "trade and aid" strategy toward Latin America.[61]

Business Internationalists and the Alliance for Progress

Business internationalists endorsed expansion of aid to Latin America as early as 1958. The CFR, the NPA, and the Committee for Economic Development communicated their interest in a "trade and aid" foreign economic policy to State Department officials in the Eisenhower administration. The culmination of business internationalist influence on the shift to "trade and aid" was the Rockefeller Report of 1958, which brought together representatives from the CFR and the NPA to advocate U.S. government promotion of increased spending for regional integration, infrastructure, and technical assistance in Latin America.

Despite the efforts of the Eisenhower State Department to influence the scope and pace of the integration movement, business internationalists close to the administration were frustrated by the lack of progress toward growth in bilateral assistance to the region. David Rockefeller's Business Group for Latin America brought together virtually all the U.S. investors in Latin America in 1958 to give political support to an expanded bilateral aid program. The Rockefeller group strongly endorsed the efforts of the Kennedy administration to implement the Alliance for Progress, which business internationalists perceived as necessary to encourage increased investment in the region.

During the 1960s, the Rockefeller group met with Kennedy and Johnson officials to coordinate public and private programs designed to encourage direct private investment in Latin America.[62] As we will see, AID officials evaluated their programs in each Central American country according to two primary considerations: whether or not the country was open to foreign investment and whether or not the country harbored an internal "nationalist" or "communist" threat to U.S. interests in the region.

The Kennedy administration created AID in 1961 within an institutional context of an "aid regime" that sought to enhance the prospects for U.S. investment in and trade with Latin America. The initial charter of the Alliance for Progress pronounced the guidelines covering the expanded assistance to Latin America during the 1960s. The guidelines allow us to speak of an aid regime characterized by particular stipulations regarding the allocation of financial assistance to the region. The Charter of Punta del Este, which established the Alliance for Progress, tells us that the Kennedy administration was concerned about ensuring increased foreign investment in and trade with Latin America. The alliance charter included a clause pushed by U.S. policy makers that committed the Latin American governments to the promotion "of conditions that will encourage the flow of foreign investments" to the region.[63] As we will see in the case of El Salvador, the expansion of bilateral aid in the 1960s complemented U.S. direct foreign investment in the region by easing the costs associated with such investment.

Despite the clause cited, business internationalists who drafted the Rockefeller Report and who composed the Business Group for Latin America wanted to downplay the role of the U.S. government in pursuing an expansion of foreign direct investment.[64] Business firms that could afford to invest behind Latin American tariff walls were mainly concerned with ensuring the promotion of regional integration and infrastructure that would complement U.S. investment. These groups felt that U.S. aid to Latin American integration would by itself generate numerous benefits to U.S. investors through improved markets and infrastructure.

On the other hand, economic nationalists represented by NAM and the Chamber of Commerce wanted to ensure that any aid programs authorized by Congress be designed to protect domestic industry against foreign competition. Domestic industrialists pressured Congress to amend the Foreign Assistance Act of 1961 to ensure that U.S. aid would not be furnished to any foreign enterprise that would compete with U.S. business "unless the country concerned agrees to limit the export of the product to the United States to 20 percent of output."[65] In addition, business exporters of machinery and vehicles succeeded in pressuring Congress to limit AID expenditures to purchases of goods and services in the United States.[66] By 1967, a study of AID showed that 90 percent of all AID commodity expenditures went to U.S. corporations.

Business nationalists close to Congress insisted that support for any expanded aid program be contingent on the extent to which the aid program would benefit U.S. producers. Scholars who focus on domestic industrialists and/or exporters in their analysis of business support for the Alliance for Progress typically overstate business skepticism and oppostion to alliance programs. Business internationalists, or direct investors, often supported the most liberal aspects of the alliance, including its funding of health and education, which they saw as essential for open market economies that wished to attract foreign investment. Economic nationalists generally supported aid only to the extent that it benefited U.S. firms directly, or on the condition that it did not enhance foreign competitors of U.S. firms.

The compromise among these different business interests was reflected in the stipulations of the Foreign Assistance Act of 1961 and in various amendments to that act.[67] What emerged was the institutional foundation of laws and regulations governing the allocation of bilateral aid.

The AID Regime in El Salvador

Business internationalists' participation in designing and implementing bilateral assistance programs to Latin America is apparent even in the country of El Salvador, where one would not expect private investors to take such a political interest in development lending. In 1961, business internationalists, including Peter Grace of Grace Lines, Leo Welch of Standard Oil, Walter Donnelly of U.S. Steel, and Wilbur Morrison of Pan American Airways, worked with AID in fashioning a development program for El Salvador.[68]

An AID document of 1964 summarized the overall objectives of bilateral aid, which centered on the "achievement of maximum industrialization for El Salvador via promotion of Banking and Industrial Institutions" designed to promote increased private and foreign investment.[69] Toward these ends, AID extended a $5.1 million loan to finance the establishment of a private investment bank to assist the private sector (domestic and foreign) with development credits.[70] AID also worked with the Inter-American Development Bank to promote "development planning" (infrastructure) consistent with the needs of foreign direct investors.[71]

Throughout the 1960s, AID officials and business internationalists worked with El Salvador's Industrial Development Institute (INSAFI) to channel technical advice and monetary assistance to support programs for foreign investment. This effort included the following: (1) review by a U.S. expert of criteria and methods of INSAFI; (2) advice to INSAFI by consultants (usually U.S. foreign investors) in specialized industrial fields; (3) efforts to create a private development bank; and (4) creation by AID's Productivity Center, U.S. private investors, and INSAFI of a corps of "consultant-instructors" to train managers, foremen, and technicians in techniques of production and management.[72]

INSAFI had made 121 loans totaling $1.5 million and an additional 93 loans totaling $903,000 through July 1963, with over three-fourths going to U.S. firms or joint ventures involving U.S. firms.[73] In July 1963, a promotional office of INSAFI opened in New York City with the hope of attracting more than $1 million from U.S. investors interested in promoting industrial projects in El Salvador.[74]

The promotional activities of AID and INSAFI generated considerable interest among U.S. manufacturers, which by 1963 began to dramatically increase their investments in the country, many of which relied on imported inputs. Alcoa in 1963 launched a joint venture to make aluminum shapes from imported industrial extrusion ingot; Lenox in 1964 started a plant that manufactured plastic products from imported plastic powders and resins; and Crown Zellerbach in 1965 began producing corrugated cardboard boxes from imported paper. Also in 1963, First National City Bank group began its branch operations in El Salvador and established manufacturing facilities with bank-related firms, including Kimberly Clark, Phelps-Dodge, and Monsanto.[75] Each of these firms took advantage of the tax credits, technical assistance programs, and subsidies offered by AID and by INSAFI.

The fact that AID focused much of its efforts on industrial development and infrastructure meant that the primary beneficiaries of the U.S. assistance program were U.S. multinational corporations. From data compiled on U.S. direct foreign investment in El Salvador, Marc Herold concludes that there was "no major industrial branch where foreign capital did not play an important role."[76]

As Herold's data indicate, most of the foreign direct investment during the 1960s went into manufactures designed for the Common Market. As was characteristic of investment patterns throughout Central America, U.S. firms began producing textiles, processed foods, chemicals, and paper products for the region. The stock of U.S. industrial investment in El Salvador alone rose from $43 million in 1963 to $110 million by 1968.[77]

The Kennedy State Department relied on AID to promote increased direct investment in the region as a central component of the "trade and aid" foreign economic policy. The rationale for the policy was developed during the 1950s by business internationalists and university professors concerned about the slow rate of foreign investment in the Third World. For these internationalists, economic growth and development depended on a steady infusion of foreign capital that would help promote the conditions for economic takeoff necessary for political stability.

Modernization theory, as it was called, posited a need for foreign aid programs that could create the infrastructure, incentives, and technical assistance necessary for expanded foreign and local private investment. Republican internationalists frustrated by the slow response of the Eisenhower administration to their proposals for economic aid found that the Kennedy administration was fully committed to the tenets of the modernization approach. In fact, Kennedy himself worked with business internationalists from the NPA and CFR in developing the outlines for such an approach in 1958.[78]

AID's marketing scheme in El Salvador and the whole of Central America reflected the influence of Walt Rostow, an early spokesperson for the "trade and aid" policy. From 1961 to 1968, AID promoted marketing arrangements in the region that provided extensive technical and monetary assistance to U.S. and Central American firms producing for the Common Market. In keeping with the recommendations of the Rockefeller Report of 1958, the State Department sought to provide low-cost incentives for U.S. firms producing for the regional market. The Regional Office of Central America and Panama (ROCAP), an AID affiliate, outlined the objectives of "Operation Market" in a report to the State Department. The objectives centered on reducing the operating costs for U.S. and Central American manufacturing firms to provide incentives for increased production at lower prices for the regional market. The ROCAP report summarized its efforts to lower the distribution costs of firms producing for the regional market by "bringing manufacturers together with brokers—where feasible, helping brokers in their day-to-day operations; by counseling with manufacturers on packaging, merchandising, shipping, pricing, and advertising."[79]

In keeping with the orientation of "Operation Market," the AID program in El Salvador provided U.S. and Salvadoran manufacturing firms with assistance in developing a skilled work force at minimal costs. AID started an apprentice program that provided considerable incentives to firms producing for the regional market. AID described this program in a classified National Security Council file:

The AID-sponsored Alliance project has succeeded in providing additional skilled labor to the El Salvador work force at a greatly increased rate and at costs considerably below those of methods previously used. A nationwide apprenticeship training program has produced in eighteen months time 1089 applicants registered in 74 job occupations at an average cost of approximately $104 per apprentice per year. This doubles the number produced by normal methods of industrial training and at less than 15 percent of the cost. 290 industrial and commercial establishments have participated and benefited from this program [through finer quality of work, less absenteeism, etc.]. . . . It is estimated that an additional 800 apprentices will enter the skilled labor force in calendar year 1964.[80]

Business internationalists close to the Kennedy and Johnson administrations helped design AID programs in El Salvador consistent with the "trade and aid" strategy for the region. The strategy was based on an expansion of bilateral and multilateral lending targeted toward development of the preconditions for increased U.S. foreign direct investment in a regional common market. U.S. policy makers saw foreign direct investment as a crucial part of the economic solution to lagging growth trends in the region. Business internationalists and intellectual proponents of modernization theory argued that foreign direct investment would help promote economic growth that would lead to political stability in the hemisphere.

AID's annual country-by-country evaluations of Central America revealed that the creation of open market economies hospitable to foreign direct investment was an important goal of alliance planners. Despite the tremendous disparity of wealth in El Salvador, State Department officials and AID planners consistently gave the country high marks in its annual evaluations. In fact, the country seemed to vindicate the expectations of modernization theorists about the relationship between foreign capital, international lending, and economic growth. In a July 1, 1964, report on El Salvador for President Johnson, the National Security Council cited it as the "bright spot" among all the countries of Central America, demonstrated by a growth rate of 6.2 percent in 1964 and an ability to attract considerable foreign investment.[81]

By 1968, this assessment had changed as the Central American Common Market began to show signs of strain under the weight of tension among Central American countries concerning the relative benefits of CACM and the increasing restiveness of labor in industries producing for the CACM. Business internationalists and U.S. policy makers responded with a shift from political and economic support of the regional market to a foreign economic policy of export promotion. Bilateral lending to the regional market was dramatically reduced in favor of private and multilateral efforts to promote exports from the region.

Through 1967, U.S. policy makers and business internationalists helped coordinate an aid regime that extended bilateral and multilateral support for regional integration in Central America. AID supported integration through industrialization and marketing programs that helped U.S. firms establish branch plants in the region. AID also channeled funding toward the Central American Bank for Economic Integration, which created an integration fund in 1965 with an AID loan of $35 million.[82] AID coordinated its efforts with the World Bank and the Inter-American Development Bank, which funded the infrastructure projects basic to integration and profitable foreign investment.

This aid regime lasted until 1968, when the opportunities for foreign investment in import-substituting industrialization began to reach their limitations. In 1968, foreign investors began to organize for U.S. government support of export promotion from Central America as a substitute for ISI. U.S. investors represented by David Rockefeller's Council for Latin America pushed for an export promotion campaign that would support the efforts of U.S. producers interested in shifting the final touches of their manufacturing operations to Central America in an effort to increase their competitive edge in the world market. The Johnson administration responded with a directive to U.S. AID that established the contours of an aid regime based on export promotion that would dominate the 1970s. As we will see in chapter 5, this shift is reflected in AID's policies of 1968, which moved from support for regional integration and ISI to support for export promotion.

5

Support for Export Promotion in Central America and the Caribbean

Following the decline of the Central American Common Market in the late 1960s, business internationalists interested in diversifying their investments in the region pressured U.S. policy makers under the Johnson and Nixon administrations to lend support to export promotion.[1]

The chapter will highlight the relative influence of business sectors in explaining the shift in U.S. foreign economic policy from support for the CACM to support for export promotion strategies. First, I will examine the historical context of the shift—that is, the breakdown of the CACM. Second, I will examine the variety of business groups involved in export industries in the region throughout the 1970s. Third, I will attempt to explain the nature of the foreign economic policies undertaken by the Johnson and Nixon administrations in shifting to an export promotion strategy.

The Decline of the Central American Common Market

By 1968, the limitations of an ISI strategy were becoming apparent to both business internationalists and the Johnson administration. Leading business journals expressed concern about the political and economic future of the Common Market.[2] Politically, the market threatened to disintegrate under the heightened tensions between El Salvador and Honduras over trade and border disputes. The strain eventually resulted in the "soccer war" of 1969, followed by the pullout of Honduras from the CACM during the same year. Later, Costa Rica would further jeopardize the Common Market by its decision to suspend automatic payments through the Central American Clearing House for regional imports. The clearinghouse, formed by the central banks of the Central American countries, financed regional trade in local currency by extending a credit line of $2.5 million to each member country.

Costa Rica symbolized the increasing difficulty of the Central American countries in financing regional imports. By June 15, 1971, the Costa Rican trade deficit with the region alone, as measured by its debt to the clearinghouse, was $22 million.[3] In addition, U.S. investors were worried that declining growth rates in the region indicated that opportunities for foreign investment in ISI industries were being exhausted.[4]

As Victor Bulmer-Thomas has explained, the ISI strategies of the 1960s exacerbated the economic problems experienced by the Central American economies in the late 1960s:

A major problem is that ISI, far from reducing balance of payments problems and foreign exchange bottlenecks, frequently increases them. The reasons are threefold: first, ISI is itself very import-intensive and new industrial activities typically generate a high demand directly and indirectly for imports from [the rest of the world] as intermediate goods, spare parts, capital equipment, etc.; second, the policies designed to favor ISI frequently discriminate against exports, so that the supply of foreign exchange is lower than it might otherwise be; third, ISI . . . shifts the structure of extra-regional imports in favor of intermediate and capital goods. . . . This was a serious problem for CACM as early as 1970 with 55 percent to 74 percent of all earnings from extra-regional exports swallowed up by industry's need for foreign exchange to buy intermediate goods.[5]

U.S. investors and government officials began reacting to the economic and political problems of the CACM by formulating a shift in U.S. foreign economic policy that decreased the level of bilateral assistance available for regional integration in favor of support for export promotion. The Johnson administration and business internationalists worked with the Agency for International Development to facilitate increases in nontraditional exports from the region.[6]

The shift from ISI to export promotion was not an abrupt change that occurred in as little as one or two years. Instead, the CACM experienced a gradual breakdown starting in 1968 and extending throughout the 1970s, when more firms, domestic and foreign, began producing for the extraregional market. Between 1960 and 1969, the average annual rate of growth of manufacturing exports was 12.4 percent outside the region, but 28.6 percent within the region. In contrast, during the period from 1970 to 1976, extraregional manufacturing exports jumped to an annual average of 22 percent, while exports within the region grew by only 6.6 percent annually.[7]

During the latter period there were a greater number of U.S. firms engaged in export production in Central America for the U.S. market, including agribusiness firms in food processing, marketing, and distribution ventures; electronics, computer parts, and data processing firms interested in cutting costs by "sourcing" in Central America and the Caribbean; and textile firms, as well as an influx of tourist industries.

At the same time, foreign and domestic production for the regional market did not disappear. Many U.S. firms such as Kimberly Clark and Firestone continued to produce for the CACM, but that market declined in relative importance alongside the growth of nontraditional export industries.[8] Other firms previously producing for the regional market shifted to export production for the North American market.

The beginning of a political coalition advocating U.S. government assistance in promoting nontraditional exports took place in the mid-1960s, when U.S. banks and agribusiness firms were searching for ways to diversify their investments in Central America and the Caribbean. This outlook contrasted with the almost exclusive focus by business internationalists on promoting regional integration during the late 1950s and early 1960s. At that time, U.S. banks, under the leadership of David Rockefeller of Chase Manhattan, were among the most important lobbyists in pushing for governmental assistance in promoting a Central American Common Market.[9]

During the early 1960s the level of bilateral and multilateral financing for Latin American development (primarily regional integration) eclipsed the level of private financing and investment (see table 2).

Throughout the 1960s, U.S. bankers and direct investors worked with other corporate groups in the Business Group for Latin America, and with U.S. policy makers in the State Department, in an effort to increase bilateral and multilateral assistance for integration, which they saw as a prerequisite to an influx of private finance in the region. U.S. financial interests often benefited directly from U.S. loans to Central American integration institutions such as the Central American Bank for Economic Integration. These loans enabled a number of banks to establish a foothold in the region.[10]

By the late 1960s, private financing began to rise dramatically,

Table 2.   Net Inflow of External Resources and Compensatory Financing
to Latin American-Caribbean Region, 1961-80.
Annual Averages, in Millions of Dollars

	1961-65	1966-70	1971-75	1976-80
Official grants and				
long-term loans	$438	$ 939	$2,636	$ 6,715
Long-term				
private capital	683	1,404	6,081	12,466
Direct investment	396	847	2,003	3,758
Loans and other items	287	557	3,078	8,709
Short-term				
private capital	-5	318	496	-2,226

Source: IDB, *Annual Report*, 1982; U.N., *External Financing in Latin America*, New York, 1965.

surpassing bilateral and multilateral assistance to Latin America (table 2). The Bank of America established a branch bank in Guatemala as early as 1957. By the late 1960s, the bank was second only to the Guatemalan government as a source of agricultural capital, providing funds to U.S. agribusiness firms in food processing for the regional common market and financing the marketing and distribution of important Guatemalan export crops such as coffee and bananas.[11]

The Bank of America opened additional branches in Costa Rica, Honduras, and Nicaragua during the 1960s. In 1964, the First National City Bank started operations in El Salvador, where it financed the manufacturing efforts of Kimberly Clark, Phelps-Dodge, and Monsanto, U.S. firms producing for the regional market, as well as agricultural producers of cotton and coffee produced for export.[12] In Honduras, Chase Manhattan owned 25 percent of the Banco Atlantida of Honduras and Citibank had 99 percent of the stock of Banco de Honduras, while Lloyds and Bank of America had wholly owned branches there.[13] U.S. banks owned more than 50 percent of the Banco Caley Dagnall in Nicaragua.[14]

When the CACM started to look less promising as an arena for investment, bankers viewed the agricultural sector with new interest. In 1968, U.S. bankers and agribusiness interests represented by the Council for Latin America met with State Department and AID officials as part of a special working group on export promotion.[15] In the meeting, industrialists and administration officials agreed that promotion of regional integration in Central America was still important, but that priorities should be shifted toward export promotion, in recognition of the economic and political problems facing the Common Market.

A survey of the business press prior to 1968 indicates that business groups, including the leading U.S. banks in the region, began to worry about the limitations of financing and investment behind the Central American Common Market.[16] In addition, political and economic tensions among Central American countries over the relative benefits of the market began to escalate by the late 1960s, culminating in the soccer war between El Salvador and Honduras.

At the same time, administration officials were concerned that previous foreign economic policies had given rise to increased social conflict in Central America by encouraging the rapid social movement from rural areas to the cities. A shift toward a policy supporting export promotion was seen as a way to check this growing trend, identified in a memo from the vice-president to the President on April 6, 1966: "With all the outside economic aid coming to Latin American countries, only 10 percent of the funds is going to agriculture, including fertilizer loans, rural college development, farm credit programs, farm machinery, seeds and improved rural technology. This adds up to about 10 percent of the new capital. 90 percent of the foreign aid or external capital is going into activities which stimulate the flow of people from the rural areas to the cities."[17]

The Johnson administration was concerned that a continuing emphasis on the promotion of ISI industries and regional integration would only exacerbate these trends, which were seen as potentially destabilizing to U.S. interests.[18] The increasing number of strikes and work stoppages in El Salvador, the country that the administration viewed as a showcase for the benefits of regional integration, helped convince the Johnson White House to shift course in its foreign lending strategies.

Meanwhile, Central American governments began to look for ways to diversify their exports in an attempt to alleviate balance-of-payments problems generated in part by the ISI strategies of the 1960s. The move away from ISI promotion by Central American countries coincided with the interest of U.S. financial and agribusiness firms in export promotion. ISI had been intended to allow Central American governments to manufacture domestically products that had previously been imported, thereby reducing dependence on foreign imports. Instead, as we now know, ISI actually increased dependence on a whole range of imports used by foreign and domestic

Table 3.   Latin America and the Caribbean: Balance of Payments
on Current Account for Selected Periods
(Averages, in Millions of Dollars)

Country	1958-62	1966-70
Costa Rica	-$18	-$58
El Salvador	- 6	- 23
Guatemala	- 32	- 28
Honduras	- 3	- 37
Nicaragua	- 8	- 49

Sources: ECLA, *Economic Survey of Latin America* various issues; official publications of various governments; U.N., *External Financing in Latin America* (New York, 1965).

manufacturers in assembly operations. Many of these operations did nothing to ease the negative balance of payments of Central American economies. Most Central American countries faced increasing balance-of-payments problems by the mid- to late 1960s (see table 3).

In response, some of the governments began to offer an extensive package of incentives to foreign firms engaged in export production, with the hope of generating increased foreign exchange through higher exports. In 1971, El Salvador became the first to offer such incentives to export industries. For firms classified as "whole export industries," the measures included total exemption from income taxes and duties on imports of machinery, equipment, and parts, as well as on imports into bonded buildings of raw materials, semimanufactured products, containers, and lubricants used in the production of exported goods.[19] In addition, these firms qualified for free remittance of their profits from exports sold outside the CACM, and they were able to "maintain foreign income from exports in special accounts in any local bank without restrictions on the use of the deposits."[20]

Under the second category, "partial export industries," firms were eligible for refunds or "drawbacks" on duties paid on imported raw materials, semimanufactured products, and containers, which were prorated "according to the percentage of the final product that is exported" and whether or not the imports were incorporated into the product within 12 months of the time of export.[21]

The third category of firms were "export business enterprises," companies that exported products purchased from partial export industries or from national producers of nontraditional or agricultural goods. These firms enjoyed exemption from taxes on the net profit derived from their export operations.[22]

Partly as a result of these international pressures and incentives, new groups of foreign investors looked toward export promotion as the road to profitability in the 1970s.

Subcontracting in the Caribbean Basin

From 1973 to 1978, U.S. manufacturers in computer parts, electronics, and clothing moved part of their global operations to El Salvador in an effort to cut costs and to take advantage of the proximity of the North American market. These firms included Texas Instruments, Dataram, Kay Electronics, Maidenform, ManExpo, and AVX Ceramics.[23] In all cases, the multinationals attracted to El Salvador were interested in improving their competitive position in the world economy relative to their Japanese and Western European counterparts.

U.S. manufacturers viewed the Salavadoran incentives, and similar incentive programs in Haiti, Guatemala, and Honduras, as beneficial for maintaining their position in the U.S. market.[24] The Caribbean Basin was especially appealing in its proximity to North America, which helped reduce transportation costs for firms selling goods to the U.S.

Most of the U.S. firms that moved to El Salvador were "re-runaway" industries that had abandoned previous low-wage havens for the more favorable economic conditions offered by Caribbean Basin countries. For example, Dataram moved to El Salvador the year it closed down its Malaysian operation. Texas Instruments began production in El Salvador the same year it closed its Curacao plant. Both Beckman and AVX Corporation moved their plants from Ireland to El Salvador to take advantage of cheap labor, proximity to the North American market, and numerous export incentives.[25]

The move of U.S. multinationals into El Salvador was part of a broader trend of corporations subcontracting to the Caribbean Basin part of their operations that produced for the U.S. market. In Haiti, 150 U.S. and 40 other foreign-owned firms in electronics, computer parts, and clothing were producing for the U.S. market between 1975 and 1981, when the dollar value of international subcontracting in the Caribbean increased fourfold. In the Dominican Republic during the 1970s, more than 50 percent of the products shipped to the United States were assembled by foreign contractors.[26] By the late 1970s, foreign multinationals were increasingly viewing the Caribbean Basin as an important subcontracting area for enhancing international competitiveness and market position.

The increased economic importance of the Caribbean Basin to multinational direct investors is indicated by the formation in 1979 of the Caribbean/Central American Action, an influential corporate interest group with extensive ties to the State Department. The corporate coalition worked with State Department officials and AID to promote increased economic assistance to the region, including the Caribbean Basin Initiative of 1984. Although there were differences among the coalition partners on the methods suitable for stabilizing the region, some manufacturers joined with agribusiness interests to advocate increased military aid to governments in El Salvador and Guatemala that had shown a commitment to protecting the U.S. investor. Joined by manufacturing interests within the Association of American Chambers of Commerce in Latin America, these multinationals, with investments concentrated in El Salvador, Guatemala, Honduras, and Haiti, combined to form a powerful interventionist coalition by the late 1970s.[27]

Agribusiness in the Caribbean Basin

U.S. agribusiness corporations, also interested in taking advantage of the opportunities for nontraditional exports from the region, joined lending agencies that helped form the Latin American Agribusiness Development Corporation (LAAD) in 1970. Bolstered by funds from AID, the World Bank, and the Inter-American Development Bank, LAAD initially consisted of fifteen corporations interested in increasing their presence in Central America through investments in livestock production, food processing, fertilizers, herbicides, and marketing. By 1981, LAAD had a stake in 173 companies in Latin America, 70 percent of them in Central America.[28] Through 1981, LAAD invested $7.5 million in livestock, 62 percent of it invested in Guatemala, Costa Rica, Honduras, and Nicaragua.[29]

Bank of America formed LAAD by bringing together corporations that already had a stake in Central American investments, including Chase Manhattan Overseas Banking Corporation, Borden, Inc., Castle and Cooke, Caterpillar Tractor Company, and Goodyear Tire and Rubber Company.[30] These corporations were connected politically to the Association of American Chambers of Commerce in Latin America (AACCLA), formed in 1967 to lobby U.S. and Latin American governments.

AACCLA has been one of the leading lobbying organizations on behalf of U.S. foreign economic assistance to U.S. corporations in Central America, including the $29 million loan from AID that helped launch LAAD. AACCLA also helped bring together investors from the southwestern United States, Central American business elites, and U.S. policy makers from southern states and the State Department to support export promotion schemes.[31] These efforts resulted in increased private investments by U.S. firms from southern and southwestern states in food processing and cattle ranching, often in joint ventures or subcontracting arrangements with Central American producers. Partly as a result, from 1970 to 1980 beef exports from Central America increased from 66,000 tons to 114,000, with 90 percent of it going to the U.S. market.[32]

Agribusiness companies were also affiliated with the Council of the Americas (formerly the Council for Latin America), which in 1968 represented 175 of the largest firms with investments in Latin America. The council worked with the State Department and AID in formulating an export promotion strategy for the region in 1968.[33] AID's marketing strategy shifted away from support for Central American integration and toward assistance to nontraditional industries producing for export to the U.S. market.

Banks represented by the council argued for greater cooperation between private lenders and U.S. lending agencies. As we will see, this was reflected in the foreign economic policies of the United States through the EXIM bank and the newly created Overseas Private Investment Corporation (OPIC). Congress created OPIC in 1969 to provide direct loans, investment surveys, and insurance to U.S. companies in Central America. Starting in 1970, private banks worked with EXIM in extending joint commercial loans to U.S. agribusiness and manufacturing firms, with EXIM assuming some of the risk.[34] By 1985, OPIC had insured $460 million of investments in Central America, including large TNCs such as Castle and Cooke, Bank of America, Phelps Dodge, U.S. Tobacco, Citibank, and Cargill.[35]

Banking in the Caribbean Basin

In addition to growth in manufacturing and agribusiness investments in Central America, another major economic trend of the 1970s was a dramatic increase in U.S. banking and financial investments in the region. In the Caribbean Basin, U.S. banking investments jumped from $1.5 billion in 1976 to $16.9 billion in 1981.[36]

The surge in banking investments reflected a number of factors. First, U.S. banks found themselves with increased international revenues following the OPEC oil price hikes of 1973. Banks sought to channel those investments throughout Latin America, with the largest borrowers being concentrated in Mexico and Brazil. Second, U.S. banks and financial institutions sought to avoid the regulations of the U.S. market via the offshore tax havens of the Caribbean Basin. In the increasingly competitive climate of the 1970s, banks sought to improve their position internationally by extending loans to less-developed countries.

Third, bankers found additional opportunities to invest in the Caribbean through the proliferation of export industries in agribusiness and manufacturing. As we have seen, bankers played a leading role in financing and directing LADD, the leading agribusiness corporation in Central America. They also lent money to U.S. companies, such as Cargill and Castle and Cooke, engaged in marketing and distributing processed foods from the region. Citibank became involved in financing the marketing and distribution of cotton from El Salvador.[37]

Fourth, Central American governments relied on U.S. banks for loans after the reduction of bilateral public lending of the 1960s. In the 1970s, private lending to Third World countries eclipsed the bilateral lending programs of the U.S. government. From 1973 to 1979, private banks lent Costa Rica $1,021 million, El Salvador $272 million, and Honduras $390 million.[38] By 1983, the total debt of the Caribbean Basin economies was $13 billion, with $5 billion owed to U.S. banks.[39]

During the 1970s, private banks evolved from a secondary source of finance to the most important creditor for developing countries. Richard Feinberg discusses the relative postion of transnational banks and other multinational investors during the decade:

As a result of this expansion, the banks—based in the United States, Western Europe and Japan—have replaced the multinational industrial corporations as the major source of private foreign capital for developing countries. In 1970, investments by multinational corporations (MNCs) in less developed countries (LDCs) were $3.5 billion, while new loans (extended primarily by banks) totalled $2.7 billion. By 1979, the banks' loan disbursements of $48 billion had far surpassed the MNC capital flows of $13.5 billion. The actual disparity was even larger since a portion of the MNC investment represented reinvested earnings rather than new flows from the industrial states. The World Bank projected that by 1990 annual net private loans to LDCs may reach $55 billion and possibly as much as $95 billion, while direct investment by MNCs will fluctuate between $19 and $24 billion.[40]

The increased economic presence of transnational banks in the Third World meant a growing political interest in the stability of Third World regimes. Since banks extended the vast majority of their loans to the governments of the developing nations, they were less concerned about the ideological orientation of the borrower than about its ability to service its debts. Banks lent freely to governments with diverse ideological orientations (from centrally planned economies in Eastern Europe to free market dictatorships in Central America). The main criterion was whether or not governments could repay, not their professed ideology.

Unlike direct investors, who were threatened by state ownership of industry and restrictions on foreign investment, bankers could realize profits from a diverse ideological clientele. This often pitted the transnational banks against multinational direct investors in debates over foreign economic policy. Although both business groups valued stability and protection of their investments, they sometimes differed over the methods recommended to achieve those ends.

In the competitive international capital markets of the 1970s, bankers were consistently willing to take risks in extending loans to developing countries as long as debts could be repaid or, more often than not, rescheduled. Throughout the decade, bankers consistently eased their terms for lending by revising upward the acceptable ratio for "such key variables as debt service versus export earnings and debt outstanding versus gross national product."[41] As Feinberg explains, bankers felt they had few options, since the alternatives would have meant "losing market shares as their competitors expanded. Perhaps more important, without repeated injections of new loans, the banks' LDC clients would have been forced into default and bankruptcy. The doctor was dependent on the health of his patients."[42]

As a result of their increasing economic interest in the Third World, transnational banks formed political linkages with the State Department through private interest groups and consortiums. Led by David Rockefeller's Chase Manhattan and by Bank of America, bankers already constituted an important political bloc in the Council of the Americas.[43] The council advised both the Johnson and Nixon administrations on the importance of shifting toward export promotion strategies for Latin America. They also pressured the Nixon administration for closer cooperation between bilateral government institutions such as EXIM bank and commercial lenders.

The Drive toward Export Promotion under Johnson and Nixon

Both the Johnson and Nixon administrations met with business officials from Rockefeller's group to establish aid programs designed to support U.S. firms engaged in nontraditional exports from the region. A memo from Walt Rostow to the President on October 17, 1968, indicated that Rockefeller's group was "deeply involved" with the State Department in the effort to promote exports.[44]

In addition, records of meetings between January 1 and September 30, 1968, indicate consistent formal and informal dialogue between business leaders and White House officials concerning foreign economic policy for the region.[45] In 1965, Thomas Mann noted the importance of political meetings with business officials of the Rockefeller group, whose support and advice was deemed essential in establishing the framework for foreign economic policy toward Latin America.[46] Under the Nixon administration, dialogue between corporate investors and administration officials would continue with some frequency, including a secret meeting between Vice-President Spiro Agnew, southwestern agribusiness investors, and the president of Guatemala in July 1970.[47]

Both the Johnson and Nixon administrations shifted foreign economic policy in the direction of support for nontraditional exports from Central America. However, the subtle differences between the two administrations reveal important clues concerning the policies advocated by business groups close to each administration. The coalition of investors who met with Johnson were bankers, U.S. manufacturers producing for the Common Market, and agribusiness interests. Both bankers and agribusiness representatives were interested in diversifying their investments in nontraditional exports, given the apparent limitations of production for the Common Market. As early as 1968, these investors were working with Johnson administration officials on shifting policy toward more explicit support for exports from the region.

By 1970, the State Department under the Nixon administration and Congress helped to facilitate this effort by extending $29 million in low-interest loans from AID to the Latin American Agribusiness

Development corporation (LAAD). By 1984, LAAD had received $50 million in loans from the bilateral agency at 4 percent interest.[48]

LADD lent its money to nontraditional exporters in the region at interest rates of 12 percent or higher. The most important U.S. borrowers from LADD included Castle and Cooke, R.J. Reynolds (via its Del Monte subsidiary), Gulf and Western, United Brands, Hershey, Borden, Consolidated Foods, General Mills, and International Proteins. The first four corporations had investments in large plantations in the Dominican Republic, Honduras, Guatemala, Costa Rica, and Panama. Castle and Cooke used the loans from LADD to help it diversify into new areas of agricultural production, including pineapples, vegetables, coconuts, palm oil, food processing, and manufacturing. The corporation invested in an array of fruit and vegetable exports from Honduras. The latter four companies expanded their fishing operations by establishihg ventures in Panama, Nicaragua, Costa Rica, the Cayman Islands, and El Salvador.[49]

Each of these companies joined with U.S. bankers in forming a powerful political coalition to support the expansion of nontraditional exports from the region. In Guatemala, the Bank of America, represented by the AACCLA, is part of over 60 LADD-financed businesses engaged in nontraditional exports. The Bank of America and Chase Manhattan are both shareholders in LADD's investment consortium.

Bankers and agribusiness interests represented by the Rockefeller's Council for Latin America and the AACCLA helped convince the Johnson administration to lend support to export promotion in the region. This did not mean, however, that the administration abandoned its commitment to the Common Market. A third coalition of U.S. investors were still hopeful of realizing profits within a regional market. These investors, including Kimberly Clark and Rockefeller's International Basic Economy Corporation, supported continued U.S. economic assistance to regional integration institutions. Comprised largely of manufacturing established to produce for the regional market, these industries were well represented in the Council for Latin America. They helped to convince the Johnson administration to maintain its commitment to the Common Market, in addition to extending support to nontraditional exporters in the region.[50]

The Johnson administration followed a dual track in its foreign economic policies toward Central America by 1968. First, the administration issued a directive to AID to give priority to a marketing strategy that emphasized nontraditional exports from the region.[51] Second, the White House maintained its commitment to the Central Ameri-

can Bank for Economic Integration by extending a third $30 million
loan to the the bank in 1968.[52] The administration hoped that this
approach would help a diverse array of U.S. investors interested in
both extraregional exports and intraregional trade in Central America. This strategy remained in place until the Nixon administration
dramatically lowered bilateral aid for regional integration in 1969.

Bilateral Aid to Regional Integration Drops Sharply

The Nixon government maintained and extended the Johnson administration's commitment to nontraditional exports from the region.
Working with the Council for Latin America, the Nixon adminstra-
tion continued to encourage AID to promote nontraditional exports.
Unlike the Johnson administration, however, Nixon officials dramatically reduced the bilateral assistance going to regional integration.

An important factor in the Nixon decision to focus on export promotion included the close relationship between Nixon officials and
the southern and southwestern agribusiness investors involved in
nontraditional export production in Central America. These investors
included Robert Vesco, who had invested more than $10 million in
Costa Rican bonds from 1970 to 1974 for agribusiness export ventures.
More broadly, these groups were represented by the Partners of the
Alliance, a private voluntary organization in which Sunbelt investors
were united with U.S. officials from Sunbelt states and regions, including Florida, New Orleans, Texas, Alabama, and southern California, and, on occasion, State Department and White House officials.[53]
The partners sought to increase U.S. investments in agribusiness in
the region, including cattle ranching, food processing, and fishing.

The Nixon administration sought to promote nontraditional exports by relying on increased multilateral and private lending. At the
same time, the Nixon government went further than the Johnson administration in reducing bilateral assistance to the region. For example, U.S. bilateral aid to El Salvador declined from $78.8 million dur-
ing the years 1962-66 to $44.1 million during 1967-71; U.S. aid to
Honduras, from $46.6 million to $43.2 million during the same period; and to Nicaragua, from $68.3 million to $56.5 million, according
to the U.S. Agency for International Development.

The reduction of bilateral aid was undertaken for several reasons.
First, the administration saw the bilateral aid program as limited in its
ability to strengthen the integration of Central American economies,
which had been the primary purpose of AID prior to the late 1960s.

Nixon officials shared the view of leading U.S. investors that the integration strategy was reaching its limits.[54] This was reinforced by the region's balance-of-payments crisis.

Eastern financial and manufacturing interests were reluctant to expand their investments in the intraregional market. Some, such as Ducal in the food industry and Clark's in chewing gum, closed down their operations entirely, "citing as the reasons the loss of the Honduran market and control of the market by other firms."[55] As Susanne Jonas put it: "These were indicators of the more general problem of market saturation in Central America."[56]

Second, international bankers were in a better position to finance new ventures in the late 1960s and early 1970s than they had been in the early years of the regional market. Financiers pressured the Nixon administration to increase the opportunities for private lending by encouraging more government cooperation with the private sector in the aid program. This meant reducing bilateral aid in favor of increased private lending. It also meant increasing the opportunities for commercial bankers to work with EXIM in joint financing ventures. This move ensured that EXIM did not lend to projects favored by the private sector and that commercial banks were protected in their lending ventures by EXIM guarantees.

EXIM also offered a financial guarantee program that covered all the commercial and political risks of transnational banks participating in cofinance arrangements. The closer working relationship between commercial banks and EXIM was a reflection of the increased lending undertaken by commercial banks during the 1970s and 1980s. Transnational bankers close to the Nixon administration insisted that EXIM must not compete with private banks in its lending programs.[57] Instead, bankers looked to the bilateral agency to complement, encourage, and facilitate the boom in private lending.

EXIM's move to reduce its portion of lending in favor of cofinancing arrangements with private banks indicated its responsiveness to the changing needs of the private sector. In fact, EXIM was merely following a well-established tenet of policy in the 1945 EXIM Bank Act, which stipulated: "In the exercise of its functions [the bank] should supplement and encourage, and not compete with, private capital."[58] In addition, the increased cooperation between the private sector and EXIM was part of the effort by the Nixon administration and Congress to bolster U.S. exports and to shore up the weakening dollar.[59]

Under the Nixon administration, EXIM joined with fifty insurance companies to enact major changes in the export credit insurance pro-

Table 4. OPIC-Insured Investors, 1979-81
In Thousands of Dollars

Company	Location	Single Coverage
American Standard International	Costa Rica	$ 496
Beckman Instruments	El Salvador	3,330
Chemtex Fibers	Costa Rica	1,350
Delmed	El Salvador	1,993
International Proteins	El Salvador	450
Kimberly-Clark	El Salvador	8,100
Shrimp Culture	Honduras	1,729
Joseph Master et al.	Costa Rica	648
Rosario Resources	Honduras	16,000
Wallis & Company	Honduras	1,186
ABA Industries	Costa Rica	63
BankAmerica International	Honduras	3,000
James L. Boudet et al.	Costa Rica	840
Crescent Corset	Honduras	635
Tri-State Culvert	Guatemala	810

Source: OPIC Annual Reports, 1979, 1980, 1981.

gram, including commercial and political risk insurance with the "same sort of deductible features common for insurance sold to auto owners in the United States."[60] In addition, a new type of insurance supplied exporters with parts, accessories, and other inventory items on credit terms of up to one year. Agribusiness exporters were able to reduce their supplier credit risks from 5 percent to 2 percent in export transactions.[61]

The creation of the Overseas Private Investment Corporation (OPIC) was another example of government cooperation with the private sector. Congress created OPIC in 1969 as an insurance policy for multinational direct investors. OPIC guaranteed investors against expropriation, inconvertibility of currency, and wars, revolution, or insurrection. In 1981, new legislation was approved that expanded the definition of "political risk" to include "civil strife, which covers more limited forms of violence against U.S. business property."[62] The new coverage was designed to cover claims of lower value—including those for windows broken as well as for entire factories blown up.[63]

OPIC has played a prominent role in insuring numerous U.S. investors against "political risk" in Central America (see table 4).

Given the fact that the U.S. Treasury backs up the insurance policies issued by OPIC, the U.S. government has an increased economic
and institutional incentive to respond to civil unrest in the Third
World that threatens U.S. business interests. Tom Barry has indicated
the importance of OPIC's increasing role in Latin America:

OPIC insurance increases the U.S. government's vested interest in upholding
"friendly" Central American governments, no matter how repressive they
may be. Conversely the United States has a stake in toppling governments
that threaten U.S. interests. The claims on OPIC by companies nationalized
by the Allende government in Chile almost drained OPIC reserves before a
U.S.-backed coup ousted the progressive Chilean government. In Nicaragua,
U.S. investors have claimed losses due to the revolution. Corporations that
have made claims against OPIC for losses in Nicaragua include American
Standard, General Mills, Citizens Standard Life Insurance, Sears Roebuck
and Company, and Ralston Purina. In 1980 and 1981, several companies in El
Salvador presented their cases to OPIC for insurance settlements.[64]

Several U.S. companies engaged in manufacturing operations in
El Salvador's free trade zone have received OPIC insurance. The motivation of OPIC in providing insurance to U.S. direct investors is to
bolster the competitive position of U.S. industries engaged in global
production and to improve the prospects for U.S. exports to overseas
affiliates. For example, former OPIC President Bruce Llewellyn justified the $3.8 million insurance policy for the AVX Ceramics plant in El
Salvador in economic terms. Llewellyn argued that the AVX plant
allowed the company to better compete against its Japanese counterparts: "In this case, it is not a runaway shop; it is simply the ability to
get half a loaf, if you will, a very important half a loaf, rather than
giving up the entire manufacturing operation to the foreigners."[65]
Llewellyn also noted the importance of OPIC insurance in promoting
U.S. exports: "About 100 of the largest companies in the U.S. account
for half of U.S. exports, and a total of 250 for about 75 percent. About
33 percent of all exports go overseas to affiliates or subsidiaries of
domestic companies, which points up . . . the fact that exports and
investments go hand in hand."[66]

The creation of OPIC and the changing nature of EXIM indicated
the extent to which the Nixon administration and Congress responded
to private sector interest in Third World investments. The administration gradually reduced bilateral assistance in recognition of the fact
that the private sector was in a better position to finance an expansion of investments in the 1970s.

Bilateral lending agencies were used to complement, not compete with, U.S. foreign investors. EXIM worked with transnational banks in cofinancing ventures that insured banks against losses. OPIC provided insurance to U.S. overseas investors in order to strengthen U.S. business against foreign competitors and increase the prospects for U.S. exports. In addition, AID stepped up its export promotion campaign by working with U.S. businesses interested in beginning or expanding their production of nontraditional exports. The Nixon administration's closeness to agribusiness companies looking to expand their investments in exports from Central America and the Caribbean was an important factor in AID's export drive.

Southern and southwestern agribusiness companies looking to enter the Central America market had regular contacts with Nixon administration officials. The Nixon government maintained close links to industries seeking to enter the Central American market for the first time. These new industrialists were generally looking to export from Central America instead of producing for the regional market. Represented by the newly formed AACCLA and the Partners of the Alliance, these companies were influential within the Republican party and with southern Democrats. On numerous occasions, they arranged meetings with Nixon officials in an attempt to gain government support for export ventures. The positive response of the administration is indicated by the State Department authorization for AID to expand its export promotion efforts, in consultation with the private sector.

A New Orientation for AID

The State Department under Nixon continued to develop a new orientation for AID that had begun under the Johnson administration. President Johnson had issued a directive for AID in 1968 that established the framework for a campaign to increase nontraditional exports from the region. In September of 1968, six representatives of large U.S. merchandising firms attended a meeting at the White House with a display of some fifty-five potentially exportable Central American products.[67] The items included footwear, giftware and home decorative accessories, clothing, fabric and piece goods, wearing apparel, textile products, furniture, decorator items, and miscellaneous specialties.[68] A large array of agribusiness products, ranging from meat to seafood to fresh fruits and vegetables, was included.

The problem for AID, discussed in a 1971 report, was the development of a suitable infrastructure that allowed for extraregional exports on an expanded scale. This meant reversing the course followed throughout most of the 1960s, when AID lent to regional integration agencies focused on improving the infrastructure for intraregional exportation. A comprehensive study completed in 1968 helped identify potential markets for Central American exports. The study focused on the following objectives:

1. Evaluation of supply conditions in Central America and selection of products for market research.
2. Detailed survey of markets for the selected products in thirteen countries (U.S., Canada, the United Kingdom, France, West Germany, Italy, the Netherlands, Belgium, Norway, Denmark, Sweden, Switzerland, and Japan).
3. Identification of potential buyers and pilot selling in the U.S. of thirteen Central American products selected on the basis of market research studies (shirts, trousers, bras, tobacco, cigars, fresh vegetables, hard candy, tropical fruit pulp, furniture components, TV/radio cabinets, veneer and core stock, parquet, flowers, and ferns).
4. A study of the appropriate form for a Central American export development and promotion institution, based on a review of local conditions and an examination of existing export institutions in the Philippines, Mexico, and Japan.[69]

In 1970, AID extended a $30 million loan to CABEI for the exclusive purposes of promoting export ventures, including the marketing efforts listed here and the development of infrastructure to facilitate an increase in nontraditional exports from the region.[70] Central American elites from El Salvador and Guatemala were prominent in developing programs for nontraditional exports. They largely agreed with the emphasis of the 1971 AID report that more should be done to develop an infrastructure suited for a dramatic expansion of exports. As the AID report noted: "Much still remains to be done . . . to provide secondary highways and farm-to-market roads for linking rural areas with the major cities and external markets. San Jose, Costa Rica, for example, still lacks a highway connection with Limon, the country's principal east-coast seaport. Sea transport designed for the specialized handling of bananas, moreover, has little relevance to facilitating the flows of other commodities. The inexpensive tramper services are said to leave the Isthmus more frequently for Europe and Japan than for the United States."[71]

Both the Johnson and Nixon administrations and business internationalists saw nontraditional exports from Central America as a way for U.S. companies to gain leverage in the U.S. market against their foreign competitors, thus the importance of opening export roads to the U.S. The expansion of nontraditional exports promised more business for U.S. firms that faced significant limitations on selling within the regional market. In addition, an increasing number of U.S. firms would look toward Central America and the Caribbean as a good location for the partial production of goods destined for the U.S. market. This was especially true for a number of electronics, agribusiness, and data processing firms attempting to gain a global advantage against their competitors for the U.S. market.

As we will see in the next chapter, these firms were part of the political coalitions that advocated increased military and economic aid to the region in the late 1970s and early 1980s, when the Caribbean Basin economies faced severe economic and political instability. During the Carter administration, there was an ongoing battle among corporate organizations and think tanks over the best method to address political and social instability in the Third World.

6
The Shift toward Economic Stabilization and More Military Aid

In the late 1970s and early 1980s, a split emerged among business internationalists over U.S. policy toward Central America, reflecting a divergence of interest between capital-intensive and labor-intensive investors in the region.[1] Capital-intensive investors advocated economic incentives and disincentives to promote U.S. strategic and economic goals in the region. Labor-intensive investors advocated dramatic increases in military aid to the contras and to governments loyal to U.S. business interests in El Salvador and Guatemala.

Business groups differed in their relative sensitivity to wage constraints in the region. Capital-intensive investors led by commercial bankers and petroleum firms were less dependent on low labor costs for profitability than their manufacturing counterparts in electronics, textiles, chemicals, and machinery. Capital-intensive investors were willing to tolerate a wider diversity of regimes in Central America given their relative insensitivity to increased labor costs. In contrast, labor-intensive investors were dependent on hard-line military regimes, which kept labor costs low and ensured profitable foreign operations.

For example, capital-intensive investors, especially commercial bankers, supported economic, as opposed to military, means to check the policies of the Sandinista government in Nicaragua. These firms characterized the Reagan administration's military buildup in the region as promoting economic and political instability harmful to foreign investors. Representatives of commercial banks and petroleum firms helped draft the Miami Report of 1984, which criticized the U.S. reliance on military solutions in Nicaragua and El Salvador.

Meanwhile, labor-intensive firms, faced with relatively high wage constraints and growing global competition from Japan and Europe, argued for increased military aid to stem the tide of revolutionary movements in the region and to weaken the Sandinista government of Nicaragua. These firms were less insulated from regime changes than U.S. commercial banks, which often relied on loans to governments for the bulk of their profits. By the 1980s, labor-intensive investors in the region increasingly sought U.S. military aid to regimes that had historically supported foreign capital and that were under seige from social movements perceived as hostile to U.S. investors.

In addition, business groups tied to the military-industrial complex and right-wing ideological think tanks joined with labor-intensive industries to form what James Kurth has called a "hegemonic coalition" advocating increased U.S. military spending and economic stabilization measures toward Central America.[2] This hegemonic coalition was close to the Reagan administration, which proceeded to arm and direct the Nicaraguan contras and to dramatically increase military aid to El Salavador.

This chapter will describe and analyze the diverse business coalitions allied with the Carter and Reagan administration's policies toward Central America. There will be no effort to conclude that business coalitions "determined" the foreign policies of Carter and Reagan. Such a conclusion is not warranted by the evidence, which suggests that geostrategic and ideological factors also were important. Instead, I have a more modest goal: elucidating the rationale for the political positions of various business investors in Central America and examining the relationship of those investors to the passage of foreign economic legislation.

The first section will examine the views of capital-intensive investors on foreign economic policy toward Central America in the late 1970s and early 1980s, and the second section will do the same for labor-intensive investors. The final section will look at the efforts of both groups of investors to promote the Caribbean Basin Initiative in an effort to increase exports from the region.

Capital-Intensive Investors

Commercial bankers close to the Carter administration advocated economic stabilization measures to control the policies of the Sandinista government, in contrast to their labor-intensive counterparts in the region, who advocated military aid to the contras. Commercial bankers worked with the Carter administration to moderate the policies of the Sandinista government after the U.S. was unable to preserve the Somoza dictatorship.

In 1978, the Carter administration had authorized three loans—of $40 million, $50 million, and $60 million, respectively—to the Nicaraguan government in an attempt to bolster the Somoza regime against advances by Sandinista forces. In 1979, the U.S. government authorized an additional $65 million from the International Monetary Fund for the same purpose. In the months preceding the Sandinista revolution, the Carter State Department hoped to be able to mediate a compromise between the Somoza dictatorship and conservative opponents that would allow for the "preservation of existing [state] institutions, especially the National Guard," while "avoiding a radical outcome inimical to our interests."[3] When such an outcome became impossible after the victory of the Sandinistas, the Carter administration attempted to influence the direction of the new Nicaraguan government with a $75 million loan package.

The loan package was part of a foreign economic strategy designed to strengthen the private sector in Nicaragua and prevent a radicalization of Nicaraguan policy threatening to U.S. business interests in the region. Transnational bankers close to the Carter administration believed such a strategy could succeed in moderating the policies of the Sandinistas and protecting U.S. investments in Nicaragua. After the Nicaraguan revolution, U.S. bankers negotiated a refinancing of $600 million of Nicaragua's debt with the Sandinista regime. According to the *Financial Times* of September 16, 1980, and the *New York Times* of September 13, 1980, a consortium of U.S. banks worked with the Carter administration to formulate the terms of a bilateral aid package to the regime conditional on the successful private negotiations of Nicaragua's debt.

During the winter of 1979 and 1980, a steering committee of thirteen bankers representing ninety creditor banks met with Nicaraguan officials to complete the task of renegotiating the massive debt owed to the private sector by Somoza. The bankers succeeded in pressuring the Nicaraguan government to repay all of the Somoza regime's debts at commercial rates over a twelve-year period. The Nicaraguan government accepted the terms of the agreement to avoid being shut off from all short- and medium-term loans from international banks in the capitalist world. The result was the delay of infrastructural improvements and wage increases for the working population so that the international banks could be paid off. In response to the international pressure of private lenders, the Sandinistas limited the end-of-year bonuses for workers to $150 in 1979.[4]

It was only after the transnational bankers and the Sandinistas negotiated the basis for a debt agreement that the Carter administration proposed a $75 million loan package to the Sandinistas, of which $70 million was credits to buy U.S. goods and only $5 million was grants. In addition, 60 percent of the loan package was targeted explicitly to the Nicaraguan private sector, with the intention of strengthening the conservative opponents of the Sandinista regime.[5]

The example of Nicaragua is useful in explaining the strategy of capital-intensive firms for controlling revolutionary movements in Central America. Transnational bankers hoped to use their financial leverage to force the Sandinistas toward policies acceptable to the U.S. financial interests. The willingness of the Sandinista government to negotiate a refinancing of Somoza's debt indicated to private bankers that the regime could be influenced by economic and diplomatic pressure. Thus transnational bankers or "liberal internationalists" close to the Carter administration argued against right-wing political groups that advocated military force against the Sandinista regime.

In July of 1980, the Business International Corporation, a corporate advisory group, expressed the views of capital-intensive investors in its Latin American Forecasting Study report on Nicaragua. The report concluded that the "Nicaraguan government seems to be gravitating toward a relatively moderate course. . . . The private sector still has an audible voice, although clearly not a dominant one. There are several functioning parties in the country, but none are expected to have the force or popularity of a Sandinista party with a good grassroots organization. It is thought by most observers that the Sandinista Party would likely win any election held."[6]

With the above in mind, capital-intensive investors, especially commercial bankers with loans to the Nicaraguan state and those investors still active in Nicaragua such as Exxon, Citibank, and service and transportation companies, advocated economic pressure to keep the Sandinistas on a moderate policy track.[7] The recommendation by investors who drafted the Business International report was to use the threat of eliminating foreign aid to push the Sandinistas toward a more cooperative policy toward foreign capital. These investors warned against using military force to challenge the Sandinistas, a course that would only serve to destabilize the investment climate and push the Sandinista regime further left.

Commercial bankers joined with petroleum interests (and academics) to reiterate this approach to Central American instability in the Miami Report of 1984. The report advocated an emphasis on economic, rather than military, aid to Central America in order to promote U.S. economic and strategic interests. The report indirectly criticized the Reagan administration's emphasis on the "East-West" dimensions of the Central American crisis and underscored the limitations of military solutions to the region's problems. In a paragraph indicative of the views of capital-intensive investors in the region, the report warned against an emphasis on military responses to the Central American crisis:

The East-West aspects of insurgency in the region, while tempting to emphasize, need to be given a proper perspective alongside the consideration that rural peasant movements in opposition to an oligarchic regime are not necessarily a function of external subversion. There is a real danger in seeing such opposition as only a result of enemy actions, which view tends to support responses such as military aid, as opposed to aid aimed at eradication of some of the basic social and economic problems of the affected societies.[8]

Commercial bankers had several reasons for supporting a foreign economic policy that emphasized economic assistance. First, most major U.S. banks have strictly enforced prohibitions against arms sales financing, based on the instability and uncertainty that can result from military sales. Also, bankers have opposed dramatic increases in military spending because of the adverse effects it can have on the stability of international currencies. Bankers are also more prone to deal with ideologically diverse government clientele, since they rely on loans rather than direct investments for the bulk of their profits.[9] Finally, in this case, commercial bankers were concerned about the negative publicity generated by Reagan's military policy in Europe, where significant U.S. investments were concentrated.

The petroleum industry had reasons of its own for opposing military solutions to the Central American crisis. Leading petroleum investors in Nicaragua, including Chevron Corporation and Exxon, had been able to maintain their investments in Nicaragua throughout the Sandinista period. As a result, these corporations were directly at odds with the Reagan administration's policies toward the Sandinista regime. The mining of harbors in 1984 forced Exxon (reluctantly) to refuse to use its ships to bring fuel into the country. However, Exxon continued to maintain its refinery in Nicaragua. At the time of the U.S. trade embargo in 1985, an Exxon executive insisted that the corporation would remain in Nicaragua for the foreseeable future: " We've been in Nicaragua 60-odd years, with and without revolutions. We will stay as long as it is opportune in a business sense, our employees are safe, and we're permitted to operate without excessive restriction on private enterprise." [10]

Other capital-intensive corporations experienced good relations with the Sandinistas, including food processing companies Quaker Oats and Nabisco Brands, multinational banks Citicorp and Bank-America, office products firms such as IBM and NCR, and five of the top U.S. accounting firms. None of these corporations was dependent on low labor costs for profitability. As a result, they could maintain their presence in Nicaragua in the face of government support for wage increases in their respective industries. The implementation of a cost-of-living wage increase for Nicaraguan employees and increased taxes on foreign firms had little effect upon the profitability of these firms' operations.

U.S. industries that remained in Nicaragua during the Sandinista period were generally opponents of the U.S.-backed contra war, which they saw as damaging to their business interests. As a spokesperson for the corporate advisory group Business International Corporation noted regarding Reagan's Nicaraguan policies, "There is a feeling that what Reagan is doing is not good for business, and that economic aid is what is needed down there. . . . Businessmen are worried that they will end up bearing the brunt of an invasion." [11]

In addition, capital-intensive investors in El Salvador, led by Esso Standard Oil Company ($30 million of investments), Texaco Caribbean, Chevron Oil, Bank of America, Citibank, and numerous transportation and tourist companies, opposed the Reagan administration's emphasis on military aid to the Salvadoran government.[12] Instead, these companies advocated an emphasis on economic assistance, including increased economic incentives for foreign direct investment, U.S. policies to alleviate the Central American debt crisis, and economic stabilization assistance designed to promote favorable macroeconomic conditions conducive to foreign investment. These firms saw an emphasis on military assistance as counterproductive. By the late 1970s, the views of these capital-intensive firms were be-

ing aggressively challenged by a second group of business internationalists in the region.

The Interventionist Coalition

Unlike their liberal internationalist counterparts, labor-intensive manufacturers with direct investments and subcontracts in the Caribbean
Basin supported "military solutions" to regional instability throughout the 1970s. By the late 1970s, these investors joined with military
contractors and political ideologues to advocate increased military aid
to right-wing governments and counterrevolutionaries in Central
America. For example, U.S. manufacturers and agribusiness industries with investments in Guatemala lobbied both the Guatemalan
government and the U.S. State Department for continued military
assistance to combat rebel movements.[13] These groups used the Association of American Chambers of Commerce in Latin America to
advocate increases in military spending to Guatemala and El Salvador and aid to the Nicaraguan contras.[14] Labor-intensive investors
dominated the leadership of the AACCLA and often clashed with
capital-intensive investors within the Caribbean/Central American
Action over policy positions toward the region.

At the same time, military contractors joined with right-wing politicians and Pentagon officials to lobby for increased U.S. military
spending in Central America. These interests organized and mo-
bilized the influential Committee on the Present Danger and the
Council for Inter-American Security, both of which drafted position
papers advocating a military response to the "Soviet-backed" instability in the region. The Committee on the Present Danger was well
represented in the Reagan administration, with as many as thirty-
three members of the committee serving in the White House, State
Department, and Central Intelligence Agency.[15]

Finally, political ideologues who had built much of their careers
trumpeting the Soviet threat were also influential in promoting a military solution. These figures operated largely from the ideological
conviction that the human rights policies of the Carter administration
were weakening the national security of the United States. Although
in some cases these individuals worked with defense contractors in
supporting increased military spending generally and increased military aid to Central America specifically, they also worked alone as

ideological mavericks committed to pressuring politicians to support hard-line policies in Central America.[16]

Considered together, these groups constituted a hegemonic coalition in favor of increased U.S. military aid to allies in Central America. The following analysis undertakes a more detailed examination of one member of this hegemonic coalition, labor-intensive investors, tracing their relationship to the Somoza dictatorship in Nicaragua.

The policy positions of labor-intensive investors were strikingly different from the rhetoric of capital-intensive investors. Whereas commercial bankers and oil interests advocated economic pressure to protect their investments, labor-intensive investors insisted that military aid was essential to secure U.S. economic and strategic interests in the region. The differences between these groups were expressed most clearly in the policy positions adopted by the leadership of the Caribbean/Central American Action and the Association of American Chambers of Commerce in Latin America.

AACCLA was founded by agribusiness groups and manufacturing firms faced with tighter wage constraints than their capital-intensive counterparts in commercial banking and petroleum. As a result, they felt more threatened by the policies of the Sandinista government, which they perceived as promoting economic uncertainty by restricting foreign exchange and by authorizing increased wages for workers and higher taxes for foreign enterprises. In contrast, commercial banks and oil firms often took the lead in drafting policy positions for the CCAA, which never endorsed U.S. military aid to the contras or increased military aid as a solution to regional instability (although individual firms within the CCAA did endorse such an approach). The positions of the AACCLA, on the other hand, consistently advocated increased military aid to combat the Sandinistas and to stabilize regimes in El Salvador, Guatemala, and Honduras.

In the case of Nicaragua, U.S. companies engaged in mining, lumber, agribusiness, and chemicals production felt most threatened by the policies of the Sandinista government. These firms, including Rosario Resources (AMAX), Robinson Lumber, Peterson Ranching, and Atlantic Chemical Corporation, depended on low-wage labor, government concessions, and ties to Somoza's security forces to maintain their profitability in Nicaragua. The firms were part of an "enclave economy" that had characterized production on Nicaragua's Atlantic Coast since the turn of the century. The term "enclave" as used here means the economic and political power of foreign companies over the productive resources of a less developed economy.

As Carlos Vilas has noted, the relationship of U.S. firms to Nicaragua's Atlantic Coast constituted an enclave economy in three ways. First, such a relationship is characterized by the "existence of an inequality or disproportion between the economic potential of the monopoly enterprises and the rest of the economy—regional or national—in which they operate."[17] Thus the U.S. firms, having access to greater economic, organizational, and institutional resources than their Nicaraguan hosts, dominated the local economy by exploiting local resources to produce capital for export to the United States.

Second, the relationship of U.S. firms to the metropolitan market (the United States) was "stronger and more meaningful than those with the domestic society."[18] U.S. firms relied on "machinery, spare parts and supplies for their operations" from abroad, as well as the importation of "management staff, technicians, and skilled personnel."[19] Often the only aspect of production that was local was the field personnel: "sugarcane cutters, pit workers in the mines, field workers in woodcutting or rubber collection—unskilled labor."[20] Vilas notes the consequences of the enclave economy for the local population: "There is no diffusion of technology or training of the native labor force. The commissary system concentrates within the company the spending of salaries on consumer goods. Nor is there any integration with complementary local activities. Enclaves are extractive in more than one sense: When for some reason the companies depart—exhaustion of the resource, unacceptable production costs, changes in the political environment, etc.—they literally leave an empty hole."[21]

Finally, the third characteristic of the enclave economy is the ability of foreign firms to acquire considerable political power through their relationship with locally dominant political factions. Under Somoza, U.S. firms were offered numerous economic, political, and institutional concessions in exchange for their investment. For example, lumber companies in Zelaya were granted access to 27,000 square kilometers of land in 1975—more than 40 percent of the total surface area of the department.[22] Rosario Resources was part of a group of U.S. mining investors that enjoyed exemptions from taxes on the importation of unlimited quantities of goods.

In addition, U.S. firms in chemicals, mining, and lumber supplied the state with security forces to control labor unrest. U.S. mining firms paid the salaries of the police of Puerto Cabezas and the lumber camps until the Sandinistas took power in 1979.[23] When the Sandinistas nationalized the mining camps in 1979, they found "fat books of check stubs for payments to National Guard commanders and lower-level officers. In some cases, these payments were simply bribery, but in others they represented additional salaries, sometimes greater than the official ones."[24]

U.S. mining and chemical firms were dependent on low wages to maintain profitability and to pay the high costs of transporting machinery and equipment to the region. Daily wages in the mining camps were often kept as low as two dollars, and workers were required to buy produce in company stores under a voucher system. For example, the Atlantic Chemical Company, which was involved in the extraction of resins from the pine forests of the Atlantic Coast, paid workers each week with checks that could be redeemed for merchandise in the commissary. The company, following the practice started by foreign mining companies in Nicaragua, imported food and other consumer goods from abroad to sell to their workers in company stores.[25]

The policies of the Sandinista government directly threatened the interests of these U.S. investors in Nicaragua. First, the Sandinistas nationalized the mining sector, including the U.S.-owned mines on the Atlantic Coast that had been economically and politically privileged under Somoza. Second, the Sandinistas declared in a decree of August 24, 1979, that the Nicaraguan state had "exclusive rights over the natural resources included in the earth, the subsoil, the atmosphere, the continental shelf and territorial waters."[26] To enforce the decree, the Sandinistas established the Nicaraguan Institute for the Atlantic Coast, a "decentralized ministry-level public administration agency under the National Reconstruction Government Junta."[27]

The creation of the institute clashed with the interests of U.S. chemical, lumber, and agribusiness companies that had dominated production along the coast. In addition to nationalizing the mines, the Sandinistas established a regulatory apparatus that had an "active policy of conserving and developing Coast natural resources, principally fishing and lumber, and protecting the environment."[28] The Sandinistas formed state-run agencies charged with creating new enterprises (often cooperatives) and redistributing resources along the Atlantic Coast, including an ambitious agrarian reform plan, which included rural credit to small agricultural and livestock production for the Miskito, Sumu, and Mestizo communities. As Vilas notes, "Rural credit to small producers on the Atlantic Coast went from 7 million cordobas in 1979/1980 to 36.3 million in 1980/81."[29]

The result was an exodus of U.S. mining, chemical, lumber, and agribusiness firms from the Atlantic Coast. Rosario Mining, Noranda Mines, the Asarco mining company, Robinson Lumber, Peterson Ranching, and the Atlantic Chemical Corporation all left Nicaragua because of the nationalization and regulatory policies of the Sandinistas. Each of these companies either lost its property directly to the Sandinista government or lost political influence under the Sandinista reorganization of the political administration of the Atlantic Coast. Some U.S. firms that stayed for a few years after the revolution, such as Castle and Cooke, eventually left because of concerns about the shortage of foreign exchange and their inability to repatriate profits, for lack of dollars.

The base of opposition to the Nicaraguan revolution came from U.S. firms dependent on political and economic concessions from the Somoza regime. Most of these firms in agribusiness, mining, chemicals, and lumber fled the country almost immediately after the Sandinista revolution of 1979. U.S. firms clashed with the Sandinista regime on questions relating to the repatriation of profits, foreign exchange control, and labor legislation. Unlike their capital-intensive counterparts in commercial banking, petroleum, services, and transportation, these firms became open opponents of the Sandinista regime and some called for the overthrow of the the Sandinistas and the reinstatement of the Somoza National Guard.

Soon after the Sandinistas consolidated power, U.S. companies opposed to the regime began to use their influence within the Association of American Chambers of Commerce in Latin America. The AACCLA was led by agribusiness interests that had long advocated military aid to Guatemala, Honduras, and El Salvador to protect U.S. investments from revolutionary instability. After 1979, the AACCLA continued to support aid to military governments loyal to U.S. business interests. By 1982, the organization was on record as supporting the Reagan administration policy of armed assistance to the Nicaraguan contras.[30]

At the annual corporate briefing session of 1982 sponsored by the AACCLA and the Council of the Americas, R. Bruce Cuthbertson, AACCLA's regional vice president for Central America, stated his organization's position on aid to the contras: "There is no future" in Nicaragua "unless the Sandinistas are thrown out." He added that the entire future of Central America depended on defeat of the Sandinistas.[31]

In fact, many U.S. firms with labor-intensive operations in Central American countries other than Nicaragua worried about the negative impact of Sandinista policies on a regional basis. These firms, concentrated in electronics and textile industries in El Salvador and Guatemala, lobbied for increased military assistance to the region and for U.S. readiness to send in troops if the situation warranted. In 1983, an AACCLA position paper on Central America urged the United States government to assume a more reliable role as "a supplier of military training and equipment" to Central American allies.[32]

The next section will overview the importance of the Caribbean Basin to labor-intensive investors in electronics, textiles, computers, and data processing. Like the agribusiness, chemicals, mining, and lumber firms in Nicaragua, these investors were an important part of a broad coalition advocating U.S. economic and political assistance to promote investments in Central America. Although not all of them advocated military intervention, they did join with other firms (both labor- and capital-intensive) to advocate increased U.S. economic aid and political support for U.S. investments in Central America.

Subcontracting in the Caribbean Basin

U.S. direct investors, especially industries struggling to compete in the world market, were among the most important members of the "hegemonic coalition." These investors, concentrated in computers, electronics, data processing, and clothing, had moved to the Caribbean Basin to establish low-cost export platforms for the U.S. market. Often these multinationals established plants engaged in partial production and/or packaging of products as part of a global marketing strategy designed to enhance their competitiveness versus their international rivals.[33] By the late 1970s, U.S. direct investors viewed the Caribbean Basin as important to their goals.

The emergence of social movements and revolutionary groups threatened U.S. investors that had come to depend on conservative regimes for economic and military assistance. For example, every Central American country had offered U.S. corporations a free-enterprise zone with lucrative economic and social benefits, including low tariffs, minimal or nonexistent taxation, and full repatriation of profits. The governments of Guatemala and El Salvador also guaranteed military and police protection against rebel movements that threatened the operation of multinationals. In Guatemala, U.S. investors in agribusiness worked with the right-wing death squad Amigos del

Pais to protect their investments against the threat of worker strikes and rebel insurgency.[34]

The largest Fortune 500 firms have viewed the Caribbean Basin as an important area for maintaining their market position in the United States. This has been especially true during the last fifteen years, when U.S. multinationals have faced significant challenges from Japan, the "four dragons" (South Korea, Taiwan, Singapore, and Hong Kong), and Western Europe. The effort to relocate partial production of manufacturing goods throughout the Caribbean Basin has been part of a global effort to cut labor and transportation costs against foreign competition.

A leading Japanese business scholar, who has worked with several U.S. multinationals as an economic consultant, describes the current global economy as a triad, identified by the competition among multinationals for market advantage in the United States, Europe and the Far East. Kenichi Ohmae has argued that the success of a multinational increasingly depends on its ability to develop communications, marketing, and transportation networks that provide links to the most important global markets. In Ohmae's view, the most important reasons for relocating production revolve around the establishment of such linkages to the triad markets of the United States, Western Europe, and the Far East.[35] From this perspective, the Caribbean Basin is important primarily for its proximity to the U.S. market. Firms locating there are able to take advantage of communication and distribution networks to export goods to the United States.

Relocation to the less-developed world is most effective when geared toward export production for the most important triad markets. Looked at in this way, the drive by U.S. manufacturers into the Caribbean Basin is not due primarily to the attraction of basin or Central American markets, which have minimal purchasing power. Instead, locating part of a company's production in the Caribbean basin is viewed as one method of enhancing the competitiveness of products entering the U.S. market.

Just as Japanese multinationals have relied on relocating production to less-developed economies in the Far East to gain a competitive advantage globally, U.S. multinationals in the 1970s and 1980s came to view the Caribbean Basin as important in the race for a dominant position in the U.S. market. This is especially true at a time when Japanese and European companies are competing with U.S. firms for shares of the U.S. market in electronics, data processing, and clothing. U.S. firms in each of these product lines have looked toward the

Caribbean Basin as a way to gain a competitive edge against foreign competition.

In a recent publication by the Business International Corporation, a consortium of business executives, economists, and advisers who offer publications and marketing seminars for corporate executives, the advantages of partial production in Latin America are described in some detail. The publication is entitled *Improving International Competitiveness through Sourcing in Latin America.* Sourcing refers to the practice by multinationals of relocating plants and equipment to less-developed countries for the purpose of exporting products to advanced markets. The authors of the business study argue that the Caribbean Basin, in addition to the larger markets of Brazil and Mexico, has become an increasingly important region for U.S. multinationals faced with global competition. The publication cites several benefits for multinationals relocating part of their global production operations to Latin America:

1) Proximity to the world's largest and most sophisticated marketplace: North America.

2) Vastly improved operating conditions in Latin America (including opportunities to upgrade technology via government assistance).

3) Increased use of export processing zones which offer numerous tax incentives and investment options.

4) Inexpensive, stable and skilled labor supply relative to other areas such as the Far East. This is especially true during the 1980s, as the Latin American countries have realigned their exchange rates and the dollar itself has depreciated relative to other hard currrencies.

5) Large natural resource pool, including the largest supplies in the world of such key inputs as energy (from petroleum and hydroelectric power); minerals (bauxite, iron ore, copper, zinc, lead and tin); and agricultural raw materials (cotton and other fabrics, grains, seed oils, lumber, pulp, and paper).[36]

The publication goes on to give specific examples of the various ways in which U.S.-based multinationals have used the Caribbean Basin as part of a global sourcing strategy designed to lower the costs of goods produced for the U.S. market:

1) An international data-services company has set up an offshore data-services operation in a Caribbean Basin free-trade zone. The cost savings of performing the data entry in the Caribbean will enable the firm to capture a significant slice of the huge commercial data-processing pie. The firm now does data-entry work under long-term contract for some two dozen major U.S. corporations.

2) A giant electrical company has combined the advantages of multiple Caribbean sourcing sites as a means to combat intense competitive pressures in the U.S. market. Faced with eroding profit margins and intensifying competition for certain product lines manufactured in Puerto Rico, the company restructured its Caribbean operations to integrate Puerto Rico's tax incentives under section 936 of the U.S. tax code with twin-plant operations in the Dominican Republic. According to one top executive, "For the right product lines, a combination of twin-planting or complementary plant operations between a CBI location and Puerto Rico offers the best industrial incentives available in the free world."

3) A large electronics multinational has built an integrated sourcing matrix utilizing operations along the U.S.-Mexico border, the Mexican interior, the Caribbean Basin and key sites in South America. The corporation's shift to a global organization based on worldwide product groups has enabled it . . . to obtain the best quality products at the lowest possible cost.[37]

As we can see, U.S. multinationals have found the Caribbean Basin a hospitable site for lowering production costs and maintaining an edge in the North American market over their foreign competitors. U.S. firms in electronics, data processing, and clothing have established export platforms in El Salvador, Haiti, and the Dominican Republic. These firms are an important part of the political coalition Caribbean/Central American Action (CCAA), which was formed in 1979 with extensive ties to the Carter administration.[38]

The Reagan Administration and Central America

The foreign economic policies of the Reagan administration should not be seen as an abrupt shift from the policies of the Carter White House. Both administrations were committed to the preservation of Central American regimes that had historically supported U.S. strategic and economic interests in the region. The Carter approach included a substantial increase in military assistance to the Salvadoran government in an effort to prevent the victory of revolutionary forces. Other authorizations of military assistance to Honduras and Guatemala indicated that the Carter policy was gradually shifting toward increased military aid to Central American governments in the wake of the Sandinista revolution in Nicaragua. The Carter administration, like that of Reagan, viewed the Sandinista victory as inimical to U.S. national security and economic interests. The key issue was never whether or not to support the Sandinistas, but how to control the Nicaraguan government so as to prevent a "bad example" for other governments in the region.

Transnational bankers close to the Carter administration believed that the Sandinistas could be controlled through economic and diplomatic pressure, including substantial U.S. government assistance to conservative private sector opponents of the regime. In contrast, U.S. direct investors in Central America and U.S. businesses with a stake in the military-industrial complex advocated a hard-line response to the Sandinista government. These interests were represented in political organizations close to the Reagan administration.

Motivated by a combination of economic and ideological interests, these groups had been advocating increased military spending throughout the mid- to late 1970s in a series of studies authorized by various right-wing think tanks. They included the ultraconservative Hoover Institute and the Committee for Present Danger, the latter with important connections to the military-industrial complex. As other analysts have documented, these groups had an influential voice in promoting a "military solution" to the problems in Central America.[39]

In addition, labor-intensive investors within the AACCLA communicated consistently with high-level State Department officials, including Secretary of State George Shultz, regarding the importance of military aid to the contras and to the governments of El Salvador and Guatemala. As *Business Latin America* noted in the April 13, 1983, issue, AACCLA and the administration by 1983 had established a strong formal and informal relationship via position papers and correspondence.[40] According to the publication, there were few issues of disagreement between the corporate lobby and the administration.

Under Reagan, U.S. policy toward the Caribbean Basin had two primary characteristics, which reflected the influence of the administration's corporate and ideological constituency: (1) dramatic increases in military aid to the El Salvadoran regime and to U.S.-organized opponents of the Nicaraguan government, coupled with a cutoff of all bilateral assistance to the Sandinista government and a trade embargo; and (2) efforts by the U.S. government and the private sector to work together in stabilizing and enhancing the prospects for U.S. direct investors in the region, exemplified by the passage of the Caribbean Basin Initiative (CBI) in 1984.

Both AACCLA and capital-intensive firms within the CCAA managed to put aside their differences regarding military aid to work together in promoting the Caribbean Basin Initiative. Both capital-

and labor-intensive firms benefited from the initiative. As the next section will indicate, corporations with an interest in export promotion were able to frame the initiative to enhance the profitability of their operations in the region. However, business nationalists close to Congress were able to impose import restrictions that weakened the export provisions of the legislation.

The Caribbean Basin Initiative

The formation of the Caribbean/Central America Action in 1979 was an important signal that direct investors in the Caribbean Basin were interested in gaining increased public support for enhancing the investment climate in the region. The CCAA brought together more than 90 percent of U.S. investors in the Caribbean Basin with an interest in increasing the level of government assistance available to foreign investors in Central America and the Caribbean. According to a leading spokesperson for the corporate lobby, the CCAA enjoyed extensive contact with Carter and Reagan officials in the White House and State Department.[41]

As a result, the group was in a unique position to influence government policy in a direction favorable to its members' interests. Unlike other interest groups with fewer resources, which had to rely on congressional lobbying to advance their goals, the CCAA had the advantage of meeting both formally and informally with administration officials to discuss proposals for the region.

The outlines of a Caribbean Basin Initiative emerged from contacts between representatives of the CCAA and the Reagan State Department, which officially announced the unilateral economic aid plan in a speech to the Organization of American States on February 24, 1982. The initiative largely conformed to the interests of business groups within the CCAA, which viewed the CBI as one of their most important political victories in the early years of the Reagan administration.

The CCAA and the AACCLA were the only two groups that had access to State Department and White House briefings on foreign economic policy toward the Caribbean Basin, and they were part of the initial State Department working group that developed the initiative. As a result, they were in the unique position of being able to shape the final outlines of the proposal advanced by the Reagan administration. The opponents of CBI in Congress then had to structure their arguments within the framework of a bill that had already been

Table 5.   Top Ten Duty-free Manufacturers Imported
by U.S. from Caribbean Basin in 1982
(Excluding Food and Tobacco Manufacturers)

Item	Value of Imports (Million $)	Most-Favored-Nation Duty Rate[a] (% of Appraised Value, 1981)
Transistor-logic bipolar monolithic integrated circuits, except memory	$45.2	4.2%
Metal oxide semiconductors, random-access memories, less than 9000 bits	35.9	4.2
Analgesics, antipyretics, and nonhormonal anti-inflammatory agents	34.8	11.8
Softballs	22.7	4.0
Fixed electrical capacitors, ceramic, multilayer, chips	19.5	10.0
Baseballs	18.8	3.1
Connectors, nonspecified	17.3	7.5
Diamonds, over 0.5 carat, cut, not set, suitable for jewelry	14.6	2.0
Resistors, variable except wirewound	11.9	6.0

Source: U.S. Department of Commerce, International Trade Commission (n.d.).
[a] This catagory refers to the average duty rate applied on the basis of value for customs purposes. The appraised value for customs purposes may vary for each article. It may be the full value of the article or only the value added during the manufacturing process outside the United States, depending on the specific customs regulations applicable. There was no information available on the basis for the calculation of the duty rates for the items listed.

designed with economic provisions beneficial to U.S. business, while the CCAA and the AACLA were able to lobby Congress for the passage of a bill with which they were already intimately familiar.[42]

This corporate coalition was interested in creating and implementing a Caribbean Basin initiative that conformed to the needs of U.S. manufacturing firms engaged in partial production of goods for the U.S. market. Key provisions of the initiative ensured that export-oriented industries, especially in electronics, pharmaceuticals, and some leather goods, would be the main beneficiaries of the CBI.

The initiative allowed for duty-free treatment of commodities exported from a Caribbean Basin country to the United States, given the following conditions: (1) that the country was not Communist; (2) that the country had not nationalized, expropriated, or otherwise seized property owned by U.S. citizens or corporations without proper compensation; (3) that the country did not provide preferential treatment to products of developed countries that were likely to have a significant adverse affect on U.S. commerce; (4) that the beneficiary country agreed to provide equitable and reasonable access to its markets and basic commodity resources to the United States; and (5) that certain limits be observed in the degree to which a beneficiary country used export subsidies or imposed export performance requirements or local content requirements that could distort international trade.[43]

Overall, the legislation was geared toward providing benefits to manufacturing firms in the Caribbean Basin capable of exporting goods to the U.S. U.S. firms thus stood to gain the most, since few locally owned Caribbean firms could afford to compete in the U.S. market. For example, the duty-free provisions of the initiative promised substantial benefits for U.S. electronics and pharmaceutical firms whose duty rates for material imported into the United States had fluctuated between 4 and 10 percent prior to the passage of the CBI.[44]

As table 5 indicates, electronics firms were clearly the dominant producers eligible for duty-free treatment under the CBI.

These U.S.-controlled and/or U.S.-operated firms accounted for five of the top ten U.S. imports from the Caribbean region eligible for duty-free treatment. In addition, U.S. companies involved in food processing and in nontraditional agricultural exports, such as ornamental plants, fish, peas, and cauliflower, stood to benefit from CBI. Other U.S. export industries that benefited from the legislation included producers of leather goods not excluded from the law (baseball gloves, belts), fabricated metals, and others. The initiative was not intended to have a major impact on the agricultural sector, since 61 percent of agricultural products already entered the U.S. duty-free. Also the CBI excluded petroleum products and minerals such as bauxite and nickel from the list of beneficiaries.

U.S. manufacturing firms in electronics, pharmaceuticals, and food processing dominated the political coalitions close to the Reagan administration, including the CCAA, which was led by a former State Department official. This coalition pushed for the CBI to provide its corporate sponsors with an export platform for the U.S. market. The CBI was an important part of their campaign, since it promised U.S. manufacturers increased freedom "to move raw materials, parts, and components to and from [their] offshore partners or subsidiaries almost without restrictions."[45] As Emilio Pantojas-Garcia points out, the CBI offered an array of benefits to U.S. producers:

The incentives provided by the CBI thus complement those that already have attracted U.S. industrial investments to the Caribbean Basin. Duty-free treatment for manufactured goods at least partially produced in Caribbean Basin countries complements the duty-free treatment provided in Caribbean Basin free trade zones on U.S. components and parts coming in to be processed. . . . This lowers production costs for U.S.-made manufactures and consequently increases both the competitiveness and profitability of U.S. products. The low and flexible local content requirement (35 percent of the appraised value, of which 15 percent can be accounted for by U.S. materials) needed to qualify for duty-free status perfectly suits the low value-added rate typical of the maquiladoras. These incentives, together with the availability of abundant cheap labor and tax incentives throughout the Caribbean Basin, set the politico-economic framework for the expansion of U.S. investments in the region.[46]

Thus an examination of the socioeconomic dimension of the Caribbean Basin Initiative cannot be adequately explained in statist or pluralist terms. Statists who focus on the actions and ideologies of administration officials and who assume a state driven by anticommunism might be able to explain some aspects of the CBI. However, such an analysis would fail to explain the degree to which the content of CBI legislation conformed to the needs of a particular sector of U.S. direct investors. By ignoring the role played by influential business groups in the development and passage of the CBI, statist theorists minimize the political economy of the initiative in favor of its geostrategic importance.

While both geostrategic and economic elements were clearly at work in the passage of the CBI, the business conflict model has the advantage of explaining the particular content of the legislation. In fact, the content of the CBI can be understood only with reference to the corporate sectors within the CCAA who pushed for its passage, namely electronics and pharmaceuticals firms that stood to benefit from the provisions of the initiative. A statist analysis might be able to account for the ends of U.S. foreign economic policy—that is, defeating communism in the hemisphere—but it is less effective in explaining the means used to accomplish those ends, that is, the specific aspects of the CBI.

Likewise, pluralists who argue that interest groups compete on a relatively equal playing field will not find comfort in an economic analysis of the CBI. First, the relationship of the CCAA (and other corporate interest groups) to the White House and the State Department was unparalleled by other competing groups. For example, the opponents of the CBI were largely human rights groups that had no access to executive branch officials and that were burdened by limited resources. They devoted all of their lobbying efforts to letter-writing campaigns and testimony before Congress in an effort to limit the amount of aid being given to El Salvador under the CBI.

The corporate coalitions in support of CBI, on the other hand, had the ability to set the agenda by working with State Department and White House officials on the specific content of the legislation prior to its introduction to Congress. Business groups were at the forefront of the policy-making process in establishing the parameters of the debate surrounding the CBI. By the time it reached Congress, human rights groups were faced with a bill that had already been drafted and was being supported by some of the most prominent business organizations and spokespersons, a fact not unimportant to Congressional representatives.

However, an examination of congressional debates over the content of CBI reveals that business nationalists also had some influence on the final legislation. Business internationalists were challenged by business nationalists during political debates over the content of CBI legislation. The American Textile Manufacturers Institute and the American Apparel Manufacturers Association joined with the American Clothing and Textile Workers Union and the International Ladies Garment Workers Union to lobby Congress, especially the Subcommittee on Trade of the House Ways and Means Committee, to maintain import restrictions. These business nationalists succeeded in excluding all textile and apparel products from the duty-free provisions of the CBI.[47]

The House Ways and Means Committee, in the handling of the trade and tax provisions of the CBI (H.R. 5900), amended the initiative by exempting from duty-free status luggage, work gloves, footware, handbags, and other leather goods (which are dutiable under the Generalized System of Preferences), as well as petroleum and petroleum products. The committee also tightened regulations on the eligibility of products from Caribbean Basin countries for duty-free status by raising the regional value-added requirements. The administration's plan required that at least 25 percent of the value of the product be added in CBI countries. The House version required that 35 percent of the value added come from these countries. Finally, the

House committee dropped the tax credit and accelerated depreciation provisions of the original proposal. All of these amendments to the CBI survived in the final House-Senate Conference Report, which was passed 392-18 in the House and 90-7 in the Senate.

The challenges to the legislation by business nationalists resulted in further battles with business internationalists over new legislation that would have expanded the amount of goods eligible for duty-free treatment. Business internationalists worked with the Bush administration to draft proposals for CBI II, which was delayed in the House and Senate amidst opposition from business nationalists. A key part of the debate pitted business internationalists in textiles and apparel, who wanted to extend CBI's provisions to their products, against business nationalists, who opposed duty-free provisions for these goods.

This analysis of the political economy of foreign economic policy under the Carter and Reagan administrations deals with a period for which primary documents are difficult, if not impossible, to obtain. I have relied instead on business publications, secondary sources, and interviews in gauging the role played by business interests in shaping the foreign economic policies of the Carter and Reagan administrations.

Despite this limitation, there is strong evidence indicating that business groups had an economic and political interest in pressuring both administrations to pursue particular foreign economic policies. The advice given by business representatives was not monolithic but highly dependent on the sectoral position of U.S. investors in the Caribbean Basin. The business conflict model, unlike the pluralist and statist accounts of U.S. foreign economic policy, has the advantage of being able to account for the specific measures or "means" undertaken by the U.S. government in pursuing particular policies toward Central America and the Caribbean. As we have seen, those measures often conformed to the interests of particular business groups with an economic stake in the region.

The business conflict model challenges the notion of "national interest" as it is commonly used by international relations scholars. To the extent that business groups are able to exert unequaled leverage upon the policies of the U.S. government, the term "national interest" conceals more than it reveals about the formation and direction of U.S. foreign economic policy toward Central America over the last forty years. This study has argued that each transition in U.S. foreign economic policy was facilitated by a combination of business

pressure and international economic and political variables that allowed for the adoption of new policy measures. This stance challenges other accounts in international political economy that have
minimized or relegated to second place the role of business groups in
the formulation of foreign economic policy.

7
The Business Conflict Model: The Relationship of Business to the State

This final chapter attempts to evaluate the usefulness of the business conflict model in light of the empirical findings of the previous chapters. The model is useful to the extent that it helps us explain the various shifts in U.S. foreign economic policy toward Central America and elsewhere in the less-developed world. The model represents an advance over other theoretical approaches to the extent that it can account for the adoption of particular foreign economic policies that cannot be explained by other approaches.

The first part of this chapter will compare and contrast the propositions of the business conflict model with the statist model in light of the previous chapters. The second part will draw upon the empirical evidence of previous chapters to evaluate the propositions of the business conflict model advanced in chapter 1. The concluding section will suggest other lines of research to further evaluate the usefulness of the model.

The previous chapters lend support to a primary contention of the business conflict model regarding the relationship of business to the state. At each conjuncture in U.S. foreign economic policy, business groups have played an important role in pressuring executive branch and congressional policy makers to pursue a new foreign economic policy conducive to business interests. In defining "influence," this study uses the hardest conditions that most case studies would demand. The empirical findings of this study support the contention that business groups were influential in the shift toward foreign economic policies of "trade and aid" in the late 1950s, export promotion during the late 1960s and early 1970s, and the passage of the Caribbean Basin Initiative in the 1980s.

Such findings challenge one of the foremost assumptions of the statist model, which argues that the State Department and the White House are insulated from the pressures of private interest groups in the formulation of foreign economic policy. The statist model would not expect business groups to be successful in pressuring executive branch officials to adopt foreign economic policies conducive to narrow economic interests. The previous chapters, although they do not prove that business groups were the only influence on policy makers, provide archival evidence that challenges the notion that executive branch actors formulate policy based on a "national interest" that is distinct from the interests of powerful business coalitions. In each of the conjunctures of U.S. foreign economic policy toward Central America, business groups communicated their policy preferences to White House and State Department officials in formal and informal correspondence. In most cases, executive branch officials discussed the proposals of business interests (indicating that they took such proposals seriously) and moved to translate the proposals into foreign policy.

Proponents of the statist model might respond that such correspondence indicates only that the state was enlisting the services of business groups to achieve particular national security objectives. In this view, the state formulates national objectives and attempts to gain the support of influential interest groups in implementing policy. Again, the findings of the previous chapters challenge such a view. In each transition from one foreign economic policy to another, business groups were often ahead of executive branch officials in establishing the economic and ideological rationale for the adoption of a new policy.

For example, the CFR, CED, and NPA all established study groups and commissions on economic policy matters, and they all made informal proposals to the Eisenhower White House and the State Department advocating a shift to a "trade and aid" foreign economic policy prior to the official decision to change policy. Following the shift to "trade and aid," the Business Group for Latin America was actively involved in U.S. policies toward the Central American Common Market. U.S. firms interested in taking advantage of Central America tariff barriers through import-substituting industrialization worked with the Eisenhower and Kennedy administrations to develop policies toward the CACM. Those policies were conducive to a dramatic expansion of U.S. investment in Central America during the 1960s.

The breakdown of the CACM limited opportunities for import-substituting industrialization and provided new possibilities for export promotion. During the late 1960s, business internationalists worked with the Johnson and Nixon administrations to secure U.S. assistance for exports from the Caribbean Basin. Each administration responded by promoting foreign economic policies favoring export promotion in the region. A variety of business groups were formed in the late 1960s and 1970s to lobby the executive branch to lend government support to their investment ambitions in the region, and each enjoyed a close working relationship with governmental bodies such as AID and EXIM.

In the late 1970s, capital- and labor-intensive internationalists clashed over policy alternatives to deal with threats to their investments in the Caribbean Basin. Their battles were reflected by the formation of the Caribbean/Central American Action (CCAA), led by capital-intensive investors close to the Carter administration, and by the Association of Chambers of Commerce in Latin America (AACCLA), led by labor-intensive investors who joined with other groups to advocate increased military aid to the region. The latter group corresponded frequently with high-level Reagan administration officials in the State Department regarding the importance of increased military assistance to the region. Both groups worked together to secure passage of the Caribbean Basin Initiative, which further enhanced the profitability of U.S. exporters in the Caribbean Basin.

As noted in chapter 1, however, business groups cannot pressure politicians to adopt policies in a vacuum. Instead, business interests are faced with economic and political constraints that influence their ability to secure their policy preferences. The following sections evaluate the propositions advanced in chapter 1 regarding the four intervening variables that condition business influence. Empirical evidence from the previous chapters will be used to uphold, modify, or negate the propositions of chapter 1.

Business Conflict and Sectoral Politics

This study has confirmed the propositons of the business conflict model regarding the relationship between the sectoral position of U.S. firms and their political position on foreign economic policy. As expected, firms that had extensive investments in Central America tended to advocate policies that would liberalize trade with the region. Represented by the Rockefeller Foundation, the CED, the CFR, and the Business Group for Latin America, these firms pressured the executive branch to liberalize trade with Central America to allow for export-led industrialization from the region. They were opposed by firms tied to the domestic market, which tended to support tariff barriers to protect their domestic investments.

Clearly, one cannot predict support for or against liberalized trade policies on the basis of industry category. Firms in the same industry often advocated a variety of political positions based on their relative involvement in foreign investment. Nor can one gauge a firm's political position simply by virtue of its foreign investments. Domestic firms with a propensity to export often sided with foreign direct investors in advocating liberalization of trade. In addition, exporters and foreign investors have joined to support increased aid to the bilateral lending institution EXIM, which gives assistance to U.S. firms engaged in export promotion for the global market. In the hearings before the Senate Foreign Relations Committee in 1954, for example, firms with significant foreign direct investment and export dependence advocated increased lending by EXIM. Firms tied to the domestic market opposed an increase in EXIM lending.

Finally, foreign direct investors were more likely to win their battles over trade liberalization and foreign aid if they could secure the support of export-dependent firms. This was not always the case, since foreign direct investors have interests not always shared by exporters. In the battle over the foreign investment tax credit, foreign direct investors were initially unable to secure the support of export-dependent firms. Partly as a result, business internationalists failed repeatedly to secure passage of the tax credit in the 1950s, facing opposition from business nationalists and indifference from export-dependent firms. Foreign direct investors had placed a high priority on securing the tax credit as early as 1952 in the Rockefeller Report on U.S. foreign economic policy.

Foreign direct investors also clashed with exporters over U.S. policies toward the Central American Common Market. Initially exporters were skeptical, if not opposed, to U.S. support for the CACM because the Central American tariff barriers were thought to pose a significant impediment to exports to the region. Foreign direct investors, however, supported the CACM from the beginning, since their interests would be protected behind the tariff walls. Exporters then shifted their support to the Common Market when it became evident that the CACM actually served to promote a wide range of U.S. exports to the region.

Another sectoral division posited in chapter 1 seems to be confirmed by this study: the division between capital-intensive and labor-intensive firms regarding foreign policy positions toward Central America. Capital-intensive firms worked with the Carter administration to use economic pressure to moderate the policies of the Sandinista government. These firms opposed a military solution for reasons documented in chapter 6. Their labor-intensive counterparts, meanwhile, had been forced to leave Nicaragua in 1979 or shortly thereafter, having lost the services of the Nicaraguan National Guard and Somoza's economic concessions, which had historically bolstered their profits in Nicaragua. The emergence of the Sandinistas threatened their existence in Nicaragua, either through outright nationalization or through state regulation that interfered with their previous investment prerogatives.

These internationalists managed to put aside their differences in their mutual support for the Caribbean Basin Initiative, but they again clashed with business nationalists over the terms of the initiative. The dispute was based on the sectoral position of the warring parties. Business internationalists were overwhelmingly involved in foreign direct investment in the region, and, as a result, supported liberalization of the U.S. domestic market. Textile firms tied to the domestic market had succeeded, however, in adding significant trade restrictions to the initiative by the time it passed the House and Senate in 1984.

Business Conflict and the Institutions of Government

The proposition advanced in chapter 1 was that business internationalists would have more opportunities than business nationalists to influence the executive branch in the formulation of foreign economic policy. This proposition holds up well under the weight of evidence from previous chapters. Business internationalists were able to use informal and formal connections to the executive branch to influence the direction of foreign economic policy from one conjuncture to the next. For example, business internationalists drafted position papers advocating a "trade not aid" approach to foreign eco nomic policy in the early to mid-1950s. Executive branch officials used the position papers to develop their own policies toward Latin America.

For much of the 1950s, both executive branch policy makers and business internationalists agreed on the rationale for limiting foreign aid: 1) increased foreign direct investment is a better vehicle than foreign aid for improving the economic viability of less-developed economies, 2) foreign aid would only crowd out opportunities for foreign direct investment, and 3) foreign aid should be limited so as to encourage, rather than impede, foreign direct investment.

By the mid- to late 1950s, important groups of business internationalists had begun to rethink the role of foreign aid. They began to communicate with Eisenhower officials about their concerns regarding the slow rate of growth of foreign direct investment. They insisted that increases in foreign aid were needed to provide business groups with incentives for increased foreign investment. By 1958 and 1959, the administration had begun to reformulate the role of foreign aid in foreign economic policy. Gradually, Eisenhower officials moved to adopt foreign economic policies that embodied a shift to "trade and aid" in an effort to secure its geostrategic and economic objectives. (The term "trade and aid" was coined by a representative of the Council on Foreign Relations in an influential 1954 publication advocating such a shift in policy.)

Similarly, business internationalists worked with executive branch officials to design a shift in AID policies to favor export promotion by the late 1960s. David Rockefeller's Business Group for Latin America (later the Council for Latin America) met with State, Treasury, and National Security Council officials to develop a shift in AID strategy away from support for Central American integration toward support for export promotion. The same business officials, joined by agribusiness investors from the South and Southwest newly interested in export promotion, worked with the Nixon Administration through the public-private vehicle Partners of the Alliance, which gave added impetus to the export promotion policies.

Finally, the business groups CCAA and AACCLA worked with the Reagan administration to design the outlines of an export promotion package entitled the Caribbean Basin Initiative, which significantly lowered duties for U.S. producers of electronics, pharmaceuticals, and some leather products imported from the region. Both business internationalists and officials in the White House, State Department, and Treasury were committed to reducing tariffs that impeded the export strategies of U.S. firms.

As expected, business nationalists lacked the political clout of their internationalist counterparts in the formulation of foreign economic policy in the executive branch. There is little evidence of business nationalists working with executive branch officials to devise any sustained foreign economic policy toward Central America. Business nationalists did frequently correspond and meet with White House, State Department, and Treasury officials. However, their proposals were regularly ignored and often opposed by the executive branch. The major exception seems to be the case of George Humphrey, the treasury secretary in the Eisenhower administration, who was close to business nationalists within the party and who had some influence in opposing any immediate shift to a "trade and aid" foreign economic policy.

Business nationalists were far more successful in lobbying congressional representatives in the House Ways and Means Committee and the Senate Finance Committee. For example, in the 1950s business nationalists, working through their Congressional connections, were successful in limiting the extension of the Reciprocal Trade Agreements Act to one year, over the objections of business internationalists and the Eisenhower White House and State Department. In addition, business nationalists succeeded in maintaining import restrictions on metals, textiles, chemicals, and other manufactured goods throughout the 1950s, despite the efforts of the Eisenhower administration to liberalize trade.

The opposition to tariff liberalization frustrated business internationalists, who hoped to pursue a strategy of export-led industrialization in the less-developed world. Internationalists used their connections with the executive branch to promote ISI strategies for Central America in the 1960s as a second-best option for foreign direct investment. After the Kennedy and Johnson administrations succeeded in liberalizing tariffs through the GATT negotiations of the 1960s, internationalists were able to pursue more profitably the promotion of exports from the region. As usual, however, business internationalists found their strongest allies for trade liberalization in the Kennedy and Johnson White House. In contrast, their business nationalist opponents found Congress to be more receptive to their efforts to maintain tariff barriers.

This general pattern continued to be the case in the 1980s with the passage of the Caribbean Basin Initiative. Influenced by internationalists within the CCAA and the AACCLA, the Reagan administration supported a more liberal trade initiative than the House Ways and Means Committee would tolerate. Business nationalists, using their influence via the House committee, secured significant amendments to the CBI that maintained duties on luggage, work gloves, footwear, handbags, and other leather goods. The House committee also increased the value-added requirement on goods to be imported from the region duty-free, which excluded some of the products exported from the Basin by U.S. firms. Nationalists, through the House Ways and Means Committee, also eliminated the tax credit and depreciation allowance from the original bill.

Why did business internationalists have more success influencing the executive branch than their nationalist counterparts? There were several reasons. First, executive branch officials have tended to come from business internationalist backgrounds prior to taking office, predisposing them to the concerns and influence of this business sector. Second, executive branch officials, like their business internationalist counterparts, are positioned at the crossroads of national and international politics. In order to advance the national security interests of the nation-state, executive branch officials are often compelled to enlist the services of business internationalists. Unlike nationalist business groups, both executive branch policy makers and international business firms have interests that transcend the boundaries of the nation-state. As a result, each party tends to rely on the other for the achievement of particular objectives, whether it be national security concerns or profitability in a foreign market.

The limitations of this study preclude a detailed analysis of the institutional manifestation of business pressure. However, the study does succeed in using extensive archival material to suggest that business internationalists were more influential in the formulation of foreign economic policy than was previously thought. Earlier studies virtually ignore the informal correspondence and dialogue between business internationalists and the executive branch. Scholars often assume erroneously that if there is no public record of business pressure, then business pressure was simply not influential. Yet, as I have documented, internationalists often do not publicize their connections to policy makers. Thus studies that examine only congressional hearings and public statements by executive branch officials may miss important aspects of the policy process.

In addition, a focus on public proceedings may overstate the role of business nationalists on the policy process. Business nationalists, lacking the clout and the informal connections of their internationalist counterparts, often engage in the most public forms of lobbying, as in writing letters to Congressmen or testifying before congressional committees and subcommittees. As a result, an examination of these public sources may lead a scholar to conclude that business had a minimal impact on policy in cases where business nationalists did not succeed in attaining their policy preferences. This ignores the extent to which business internationalists were successful in the policy process through the use of more informal connections to policy makers.

A fair criticism of the business conflict model is the extent to which the model ignores other pressure groups that may be influential in U.S. foreign economic policy. Certainly the influence of labor organizations has been important at various conjunctures in U.S. policy. One of the best examples is the CBI, which was restricted by the combined pressure of business nationalists and labor unions such as the American Clothing and Textile Workers Union and the International Ladies Garment Workers Union. However, I did not find a single instance in this study where labor played a successful independent role in pressuring the executive branch or Congress to adopt a new approach to U.S. foreign economic policy. On the other hand, corporations and business organizations on numerous occasions acted independently (and successfully) in advocating a significant change in the direction of policy. In addition, business has outspent labor 46-to-1 in lobbying Congress in recent years—some indication of the potential for business dominance in the policy-making process.

The Business Conflict Model and National Security

The propositions advanced in chapter 1 predicted that the executive branch would gain influence relative to Congress during times of tight bipolarity, or greater East-West conflict. Business internationalists also were thought to gain influence in U.S. foreign economic policy during periods of heightened global tension, given their connections to the excecutive branch. Both propositions appear to be supported, with some modifications, by the evidence of the previous chapters.

In the early 1960s, the Kennedy administration took the lead in developing the most comprehensive foreign aid package toward Latin America, the Alliance for Progress. The administration moved U.S. foreign economic policy decisively away from "trade not aid" toward a policy of "trade and aid" toward the region, continuing on a grand scale a trend begun during the last two years of the Eisenhower administration. The rationale for the increased assistance was the threat of the cold war and the ideological, political, and economic costs of competing with the Soviet Union around the globe. This was especially important in Latin America, given the proximity of the region and its geostrategic importance to the United States.

The increased role of the Kennedy administration in administering an ambitious foreign aid program was compatible with, and advocated by, business internationalists who had a stake in foreign direct investments in Latin America. The heightened global tensions of the late 1950s and early 1960s created a geostrategic environment conducive to the increased participation of business internationalists in foreign economic policy. This is contrary to most analyses of the Alliance for Progress, which perceive a tension between the programs of the Kennedy administration and business elites. Instead, business internationalists shared the commitment of the Kennedy administration to a greater role for foreign aid.

As early as 1958, business groups led by the NPA, the CED, and David Rockefeller's Business Group for Latin America drafted policy recommendations that advocated a shift toward greater foreign assistance. The rationale was that the U.S. government would have to assume a greater international role in promoting the preconditions for increased foreign direct investment. That role meant promoting bilateral lending programs that targeted money for the construction of roads, bridges, communications, and electrical equipment needed to spur foreign investment.

In addition, the U.S. government would channel assistance to regional development banks that provided aid and incentives for foreign investment. Both the Inter-American Development Bank and the Central American Bank for Economic Integration offered significant assistance to U.S. investors. Business internationalists worked with the administration to develop, design, and administer the programs of these institutions to facilitate U.S. investment in the Central American Common Market. The result was the creation of numerous preconditions and incentives that led to a dramatic growth in U.S. direct investment in Central America.

The context of tight bipolarity enhanced the ability of the Kennedy administration to pursue its ambitious foreign policy agenda. Business nationalists who would otherwise have opposed increased foreign aid joined with internationalists in supporting the Alliance for Progress. The result was a bipartisan consensus that emerged from the shared anticommunist ideology of the period. Most important, business internationalists close to the executive branch gained greater influence in foreign economic policy.

Again during the late 1970s and early 1980s, labor-intensive U.S. investors in Central America were part of a coalition that gained increased influence in U.S. foreign economic policy as a result of the cold war. In addition, both capital- and labor-intensive U.S. investors were able to work with the Reagan administration to develop and implement the Caribbean Basin Initiative. Internationalists during the cold war were able to gain leverage over domestic opponents of foreign assistance, given the ideological consensus over a response to Soviet aggression. The interests of labor-intensive U.S. foreign investors were compatible with the increased military spending of the Reagan administration, despite the opposition of other sectors of U.S. capital to Reagan's foreign policy.

An important corrective to the business conflict model is the inadequate attention given to the emergence of human rights interest groups during the late 1970s and early 1980s. These organizations gained some influence in U.S. foreign policy as a result of the U.S. defeat in the Vietnam War. The Vietnam War promoted significant public debate over the assumptions and goals of U.S. policy for the first time since the 1930s. The Vietnam syndrome was a recognition among some sectors of the foreign policy elite that military force does not always secure the desired objectives. As a result, political and business elites split on the best method to preserve U.S. interests in the world. That split allowed human rights groups, some initially organized to stop the Vietnam War, to mobilize against U.S. intervention in Central America.

The split between capital- and labor-intensive U.S. investors was an economic division that was part of a broader ideological debate among U.S. elites over the methods necessary to preserve U.S. hegemony. Liberal internationalists within the Council on Foreign Relations sought to steer U.S. policy away from military confrontation toward economic and political diplomacy. That split was evident in the case of U.S. intervention in Central America, especially in the debates over aid to the Nicaraguan contras.

Class Conflict and Instability

The first chapter argued that business internationalists and political elites would be influenced by the rise of leftist insurgencies in the

less-developed world. Business coalitions would advocate responses
to class conflict and instability based on the nature of their investments. There is some evidence of this proposition in chapter 6. A full
evaluation awaits the examination of now classified documents from
the period.

Nonetheless, we can safely say that business coalitions divided
on the best foreign policy responses to the Nicaraguan revolution
and to the civil war in El Salvador. Commercial bankers whose investments were concentrated in loans to the Nicaraguan state advocated economic, as opposed to military, pressure to check the policies
of the Sandinistas. They were joined by other captial-intensive investors who were less affected by regime changes than were their labor-
intensive counterparts. These investors emphasized an economic response to class conflict within the region.

In contrast, an examination of the investment history of the
Nicaraguan Atlantic Coast indicates that U.S. labor-intensive investors had relationships with Somozan security forces that allowed
them to control labor unrest. In addition, these firms, including mining, agribusiness, lumber, and chemical companies, were dependent
for profitability on significant economic concessions offered by the
Somoza government. The Sandinistas interfered with these concessions by the adoption of nationalization and regulatory policies. As a
result, these firms supported U.S. military aid to overthrow the Sandinista regime. They were joined by electronics and textile firms that
had a stake in export promotion throughout the region and were
concerned about the "bad example" of the Sandinista government.

The degree to which these business groups had a significant impact on the foreign policies of the Carter and Reagan administrations'
is open to conjecture. In the case of the Carter administration, commercial bankers were clearly an important coalition that influenced
the terms and conditions of the initial loan to Nicaragua. Labor-
intensive investors seemed to have less influence on the policies of
the administration. However, it is possible that the Carter White
House would have adopted a more militaristic response as the crisis
intensified. Evidence of such a possibility is the extension of military
assistance to El Salvador in the wake of the Nicaraguan revolution.

Labor-intensive investors dominant within the AACCLA leadership seemed to have more influence with the Reagan administration.
The organization communicated its members' policy preferences for
increased military aid to the administration in the early 1980s, and the
administration responded positively to their appeals. However, nu-

merous other pressures on the administration make it difficult to gauge the impact of the AACCLA.

First, the Committee on the Present Danger, dominated by right-wing ideologues and representatives of the military-industrial complex, were well represented in the Reagan administration. The organization emphasized the East-West aspects of the Central American crisis and urged a military response on the basis of geostrategic and ideological concerns. In addition, other right-wing organizations, such as the Council for Inter-American Security, also emphasized the geostrategic and ideological threat posed by Soviet intervention in Central America. There is no indication that this group was motivated by economic interests in the region. Finally, numerous Reagan administration officials in the White House, State Department, National Security Council, and the CIA were right-wing ideologues who viewed the Central American crisis as Soviet-inspired. Their responses may have been dominated, as some analysts contend, by their ideological orientation rather than by their connections to U.S. business interests.

Despite these caveats, both capital- and labor-intensive investors appeared to have a significant impact on the drafting of CBI. The initiative was tailored to promote the export interests of firms represented in CCAA and the AACCLA, which actively lobbied the administration for introduction of the legislation. These corporate bodies, especially the CCAA, also took the lead in drafting key provisions of the initiative as early as 1979 and 1980, well before the initiative was proposed by the Reagan administration.

In the case of both the Carter and Reagan administrations, the underlying objective was to preserve the state apparatus and military structures of governments loyal to U.S. geostrategic and economic interests in Central America. Both administrations sought to defeat leftist insurgencies that threatened U.S. business interests. At the same time, both labor- and capital-intensive investors agreed on the goal of preventing the emergence of Central American regimes that would challenge U.S. economic and strategic interests in the region. The debates over U.S. foreign economic policy did not reflect a fundamental disagreement about the objectives of U.S. policy. Instead, political and business elites differed over the methods necessary to achieve established goals. As Jonas notes:

Lest the intensity of the debate obscure the underlying unity of objectives, let us be clear from the outset: all parties were in complete agreement that the United States must preserve maximum control over Nicaragua (within the

context of declining U.S. power worldwide); the debate was merely about
how best to achieve that objective. Because the stakes were high, the tactical
debate was intense, but at no time was this underlying objective questioned.[1]

Other Applications of the Business Conflict Model

For the most part, this study limits the business conflict model to an
examination of shifts in foreign economic policy toward Central America. Applications of the model to an examination of U.S. foreign economic policy in Africa and Asia would be useful in gauging its explana-
tory power.[2] Case studies of U.S. policy in other regions would help to
illuminate the situations in which the business conflict model could be
profitably employed. In addition, comparative studies would suggest
the circumstances where the model is less useful than statist or pluralist explanations of policy.

Case studies of U.S. foreign economic policy toward Western Europe have already shown business to be an important player in the
adoption of particular policies such as the Marshall Plan.[3] An application of the business conflict model to European countries might allow
for additional insights regarding U.S. foreign economic policy. Case
studies of Western Europe would allow for a more detailed explica-
tion of the relationship between business internationalists and national security concerns. Such studies would be especially useful now
that declassified documents from the 1940s and 1950s are more widely
available.

The use of the business conflict model is not meant to dismiss statist explanations. In fact, there are occasions when these models could
work together to fashion reasonable explanations of U.S. foreign economic policy. For example, statists in particular cases might be able to
account for overall objectives of U.S. policy, i.e. to defeat communism,
while the business conflict model would be useful in explaining the
particular methods or policies used to attain the policy-making objectives. The business conflict model posits that there has been a closer
relationship between national security objectives and business interests than statists have previously admitted. A comparison of case studies would provide a more detailed analysis of this contention.

Notes

1. Explaining U.S. Foreign Economic Policy

1. See Charles Lindblom, *Politics and Markets* (New York: Basic Books, 1977). Lindblom modifies his earlier pluralist analysis, concluding that business is a privileged actor in the formulation and implementation of public policy. See especially the chapter "The Privileged Position of Business," pp. 170-213. In the area of foreign economic policy, recent pluralist works focus on business influence on U.S. trade policy, including I.M. Destler and John S. Odell, *Anti-Protection: Changing Forces in United States Trade Politics* (Washington: Institute for International Economics, 1987) and Helen Milner, *Resisting Protectionism* (Princeton, N.J.: Princeton Univ. Press, 1988).

2. Most pluralists remain committed to the view that business does not enjoy "any particular advantages" in policy making. See David Vogel, "The New Political Science of Corporate Power," *Public Interest* no. 87 (1987): 63-64. This traditional pluralist view is most influenced by Raymond Bauer, Ithiel de Sola Pool, and Lewis Anthony Dexter, *American Business and Public Policy* (New York: Atherton, 1963). On the the problem of translating economic power into political influence, see Joanne Gowa, "Subsidizing American Corporate Expansion Abroad: Pitfalls in the Analysis of Public and Private Power," *World Politics*, vol. 37, no. 2, pp. 180-203 1985.

3. The most well-known marxist formulation of this view is Fred Block, "The Ruling Class Does Not Rule: Notes on the Marxist Theory of the State," *Socialist Revolution* 7, no. 3 (1977). See also David Gold, Clarence Lo, and Erik Olin Wright, "Recent Developments in the Marxist Theory of the Capitalist State," *Monthly Review* 27, no. 5 (1975). Each of these formulations was influenced by Nicos Poulantzas, *Political Power and Social Classes* (London: New Left Books, 1969). For a recent discussion and critique of this literature, see Scott McNall, Rhonda Levine, and Rick Fantasia, eds., *Bringing Class Back In* (Boulder, Colo.: Westview Press, 1991).

4. Two examples in the realist tradition include David Lake, *Power, Pro-*

tection and Free Trade (Ithaca: Cornell University Press, 1988), and Joseph Grieco, *Cooperation Among Nations* (Ithaca: Cornell University Press, 1990). A marxist variant of this approach is Fred Block, *The Origins of International Economic Disorder* (Berkeley: University of California Press, 1977).

5. For society-centered approaches using the pluralist framework, see Stephen D. Cohen, *The Making of United States International Economic Policy* (New York: Praeger, 1988), and Chidozie Ogene, *Interest Groups and the Shaping of Foreign Policy* (New York: St. Martin's Press, 1983). From a power elite perspective, see William Domhoff, *The Power Elite and the State* (New York: Walter de Gruyter, 1990). For a marxist perspective, see Lawrence Shoup and William Minter, *Imperial Brain Trust: The Council on Foreign Relations and United States Foreign Policy* (New York: Monthly Review Press, 1977).

6. The business conflict model is a variant of the framework used by David Gibbs, *The Political Economy of Third World Intervention* (Chicago: Univ. of Chicago Press, 1991). The model developed in this study is also influenced by the following works: Thomas Ferguson, "From Normalcy to New Deal: Industrial Structure, Party Competition, and American Public Policy in the Great Depression," *International Organization* 38 (Winter 1984): 41-93; Peter Gourevitch, *Politics in Hard Times* (Ithaca: Cornell University Press, 1986); Jeffrey Frieden, *Debt, Development and Democracy* (Princeton, N.J.: Princeton University Press, 1991); and James Kurth, "The Political Consequences of the Product Cycle," *International Organization* 33 (Winter 1979): 1-34.

7. For an early elaboration of this view, see Stephen Krasner, *Defending the National Interest* (Princeton N.J.: Princeton University Press, 1978). Also see Theda Skocpol, "Bringing the State Back In," in Peter Evans, Dietrich B. Rueschemeyer, and Theda Skocpol, eds., *Bringing the State Back In* (London: Cambridge University Press, 1985), pp. 3-37. For a theoretical elaboration of the statist perspective, see David Lake, "Toward a Realist Theory of State Action," *International Studies Quarterly* 33, no. 4 (Dec. 1989): 457-74.

8. For an application of statist theory to Latin America, see Cole Blaiser, *The Hovering Giant: U.S. Responses to Revolutionary Change in Latin America* (Pittsburgh: University of Pittsburgh Press, 1976). For institutional perspectives that emphasize bureaucratic politics, see Abraham Lowenthal, *The Dominican Intervention* (Cambridge: Harvard Univ. Press, 1972), and Dario Moreno, *U.S. Policy in Central America: The Endless Debate* (Miami: Florida International Univ., 1990).

9. For a useful summary of the society-centered literature, see G. John Ikenberry, David A. Lake, and Michael Mastanduno, "Introduction: Explaining American Foreign Economic Policy," in Ikenberry et.al., *The State and American Foreign Economic Policy* (New York: Cornell University Press, 1988), pp. 1-32.

10. For example, see Peter Gourevitch, "The Second Image Reversed," *International Organization* 32 (Autumn 1978): 881-912. Also see his *Politics in Hard Times* (Ithaca: Cornell University Press, 1986), 55-60.

11. A classic work on collective action is Mancur Olson, *The Logic of Collective Action: Public Goods and the Theory of Groups* (Cambridge: Harvard University Press, 1965). Also see Russell Hardin, *Collective Action* (Baltimore: Johns Hopkins University Press, 1982).

12. For a sophisticated marxist account of U.S. foreign policy, see Morris Morley, *The Imperial State and Revolution: United States and Cuba, 1952-1986* (Cambridge: Cambridge University Press, 1987). For a historical account that combines marxist and bureaucratic approaches, see Joan Hoff Wilson, *American Business and Foreign Policy* (Lexington: University Press of Kentucky, 1971). For a recent application of this marxist and bureaucratic theory to U.S. intervention in Vietnam, see Paul Joseph, *Cracks in the Empire: State Politics in the Vietnam War* (New York: Columbia University Press, 1987).

13. For a sophisticated pluralist account of U.S. foreign policy toward Latin America, see Lars Schoultz, *Human Rights and United States Policy Toward Latin America* (Princeton, N.J.: Princeton University Press, 1981).

14. This study builds on literature that explains the ability of business interests to overcome collective action problems that burden ordinary voters. I am especially influenced by Thomas Ferguson's "investment theory of political parties," expounded in his "Party Realignment and the American Industrial Structure: The Investment Theory of Political Parties in Historical Perspective," in Paul Zarembka, ed., *Research in Political Economy*, vol. 6 (Greenwich, Conn.: JAI Press, 1983).

15. For a summary of these connections, see William Domhoff, *The Power Elite and the State* (New York: Walter de Gruyter, Inc., 1990) For the development of a theoretical model and considerable empirical research on the nature of these connections, see Ferguson, "Party Realignment." For a discussion of the historical connection of international bankers to U.S. foreign policymakers, see Jeffrey Frieden, "Sectoral Conflict and U.S. Foreign Economic Policy, 1914-1940," *International Organization* 42, no. 1 (Winter 1988), pp. 59-90.

16. Tom McCormick, *America's Half-Century: United States Foreign Policy in the Cold War* (Baltimore: Johns Hopkins University Press, 1989), 12-13.

17. Schoultz, 100.

18. For a discussion of these organizations, see Sylvia Maxfield and James Nolt, "Protectionism and the Internationalization of Capital: U.S. Sponsorship of Import Substitution Industrialization in the Philippines, Turkey and Argentina," *International Studies Quarterly* 34 (March 1990): 49-81.

19. Schoultz, 66-67.

20. On the historical influence of business nationalists in the National Association of Manufacturers, see Philip Burch, "The NAM as an Interest Group," in *Politics and Society*, Fall 1983, pp. 97-130. Burch concludes that business nationalists have vied with internationalists for dominance of this organization, but that nationalist firms were dominant during the late 1940s through the 1950s.

21. For a discussion of the lobbying strategies adopted by business firms, see Gibbs, 31-32.

22. Milner, 22.

23. Ibid.

24. Ibid., 21-24. Also see Gourevitch, 35-68.

25. Most studies have argued for a statist interpretation of the creation of the Central American Common Market. For example, see John Weeks, *The*

Economies of Central America (New York: Holmes and Meier, 1985). Weeks concludes that U.S. companies were already so dominant in the region that they had little to gain by supporting a Common Market. This study challenges that view by relying on archival sources that show that business groups actively lobbied for the CACM throughout the mid- to late 1950s.

26. The theoretical framework for this distinction comes from Ferguson.

27. James Kurth, "The United States and Central America: Hegemony in Historical and Comparative Perspective" in *Central America: International Dimensions of the Crisis*, ed. Richard Feinberg (New York: Holmes and Meier, 1982).

28. For a detailed account of the political connections of the Committee on the Present Danger, see Jerry Sanders, *Peddlers of Crisis* (Boston: South End Press, 1983).

29. For a concise summary of these views, see *The Miami Report: Recommendations on United States Policy Toward Latin America and the Caribbean* (Miami: University of Miami, 1983).

30. For a statist interpretation of the act and a discussion of the literature, see Stephen Haggard, "The Institutional Foundations of Hegemony: Explaining the Reciprocal Trade Agreements Act of 1934" in *The State and American Foreign Economic Policy*, eds. G. John Ikenberry, David A. Lake, and Michael Mastanduno (Ithaca, N.Y.: Cornell Univ. Press, 1988).

31. Robert Pastor, *Congress and the Politics of U.S. Foreign Economic Policy, 1929-1976* (Berkeley: University of California Press, 1980), 162.

32. Ibid., 163.

33. Ibid.

34. For example, see I.M. Destler, *American Trade Politics: System Under Stress* (Washington, D.C., and New York: Institute for International Economics and the Twentieth Century Fund, 1986), and Robert Baldwin, *The Political Economy of U.S. Import Policy* (Cambridge: MIT Press, 1985).

35. For a good exposition of ideological conflict among bureaucratic actors in U.S. foreign policy toward Central America during the Carter, Reagan, and Bush periods, see Dario Moreno, *U.S. Policy in Central America: The Endless Debate* (Miami: Florida International Univ., 1990).

36. For a theoretical exposition of this view, see James Petras and Morris Morley, *U.S. Hegemony Under Siege* (New York: Verso Press, 1990).

37. See Richard Feinberg, *The Intemperate Zone: The Third World Challenge to U.S. Foreign Policy* (New York: W.W. Norton and Co., 1983).

38. Gibbs, 5.

39. See Joanne Gowa, "Subsidizing American Corporate Expansion Abroad: Pitfalls in the Analysis of Public and Private Power" in *World Politics*, vol. 37, no. 2, pp. 180-203 1985.

2. The "Trade Not Aid" Strategy for Third World Industrialization

1. Sylvia Maxfield and James Nolt, "Protectionism and the Internationalization of Capital: U.S. Sponsorship of Import Substitution Industrializ-

ation in the Philippines, Turkey and Argentina," *International Studies Quarterly* 34 (March 1990): 57.

2. Ibid.

3. Ibid., 55-56.

4. Ibid., 56.

5. Ibid.

6. Council on Foreign Relations, *Studies of American Interests in the War and the Peace: Economic and Financial Series*, E-B, 67: 1-2.

7. See Tom McCormick's discussion in *America's Half Century: United States Foreign Policy in the Cold War* (Baltimore and London: Johns Hopkins Press, 1989), 12-16. Also see Lawrence Shoup and William Minter, *Imperial Brain Trust* (New York: Monthly Review Press, 1977).

8. Council on Foreign Relations.

9. Ibid., 2.

10. Ibid.

11. Robert Wood, *From Marshall Plan to Debt Crisis* (Berkeley: University of California Press, 1986), 94-138.

12. Maxfield and Nolt, 56.

13. Ibid., 61.

14. Ibid., 56.

15. Ibid.

16. Ibid., 57.

17. Ibid., 58. According to the authors, the Truman administration regularly consulted with internationalists in the NFTC and the NPA regarding favorable tax changes, elimination of laws discriminating against foreign investment, and treaties of friendship, commerce, and navigation in Third World countries as part of the Point Four effort. As I will document in the case of El Salvador, U.S. officials worked with Salvadoran officials to create the conditions for direct foreign investment.

18. David Rockefeller, Report to the Office of Inter-American Affairs, RG-59, Records of the Office of Inter-American Affairs, 1952-1953, Subject File, Business Advisory Council Folder. National Archives of the United States.

19. Ibid.

20. International Development Advisory Board, *Partners in Progress: A Report to the President* (Washington, D.C.: U.S. Government Printing Office, 1951), 79.

21. Wood, 46.

22. Ibid., 114.

23. Jerome Levinson and Juan de Onis, *The Alliance that Lost Its Way* (Chicago: Quadrangle Books, 1972), 37.

24. Joanne Gowa, "Subsidizing American Corporate Expansion Abroad: Pitfalls in the Analysis of Public and Private Power," *World Politics* 37 (1985): 190.

25. International Development Advisory Board, 86.

26. State Department report to Business Advisory Council, "United States Relations with Latin America," June 5, 1953, RG-59, Records of the State Department, BAC Folder, National Archives of the United States.

27. Ibid.

28. A Report to the National Security Council by the Executive Secretary, "U.S. Objectives and Courses of Action with Respect to Latin America," labeled Top Secret, March 18, 1953, Eisenhower Library, National Security Council, Latin American File.

29. Ibid.

30. Ibid.

31. Ibid.

32. "A Preview of the United States Position at the Rio Conference" *Department of State Bulletin* 31 (Nov. 8, 1954), 688, cited in David Landry, "United States Interests in Central America: A Case Study of Policies Toward Economic Integration and Development from 1952 to 1968," unpublished dissertation, University of Notre Dame, 1972, p. 70.

33. *New York Times*, Nov. 8, 1954, p. 8.

34. See the *Bretton Woods Agreements Act*, Hearings before the House Committee on Banking and Currency, 79th Cong., 1st sess., 644-45. Also see David McLellan and Charles Woodhouse, "The Business Elite and Foreign Policy," *Western Political Quarterly* 13 (March 1960).

35. David Baldwin, *Economic Development and American Foreign Policy*, (Chicago: University of Chicago Press, 1966).

36. The World Bank, *The World Bank Group in the Americas* (Washington, D.C.: GPO, 1972), 43-49.

37. McLellan and Woodhouse, 185-88.

38. Baldwin, 215.

39. Maxfield and Nolt, 57.

40. Ibid.

41. Ibid.

42. William Mallalieu, *British Reconstruction and American Policy* (New York: Scarecrow Press, 1956), 196.

43. Maxfield and Nolt, 57.

44. Ibid., 59.

45. See individual responses by business members of the council in Records of the Office of Inter-American Affairs, 1952-1953, Subject File, BAC Folder, RG-59, General Records of the State Department, National Archives of the United States.

46. Ibid.

47. Chronicle of Inter-Departmental Memoranda regarding Point Four Program, Records of the Office of Middle American Affairs, 1947-1956, Subject File, Box 4, RG-59, General Records of the State Department, National Archives of the United States.

48. Memo from U.S. ambassador to Raymond G. Leddy, June 30, 1953, ibid.

49. Ibid.

50. Memo from Raymond G. Leddy of Office of Middle American Affairs to U.S. ambassador in El Salvador, March 6, 1953, ibid.

51. Ibid. Note in the same memo the importance placed upon loans from the World Bank (financing for the hydroelectric project that will allow for the "expansion of industry") and the EXIM bank, which extended loans to facilitate the completion of industrial projects in El Salvador throughout the 1950s. Bilateral assistance would increase with the further expansion of U.S. industry in the 1960s, as I will document in chapter 4.

52. Memo from U.S. Ambassador Robert C. Hill to Henry Holland, Assistant Secretary of State for Inter-American Affairs, regarding nature of technical assistance to El Salvador, Feb. 7, 1955, Records of the Assistant Secretary for Inter-American Affairs (Henry F. Holland), 1953-1956, Box 6, Subject File, RG-59, General Records of the State Department, National Archives of the United States.

53. Ibid.

54. Ibid.

55. Ibid.

56. For a survey of business interest in Point Four programs in Latin America, see Records of the Office of Inter-American Affairs, Business Advisory Council Folder, RG-59, General Records of the State Department, National Archives of the United States.

57. "How to Make Capitalists Out of Coffee: A Good Recipe from El Salvador," *Fortune*, June 1950, p. 73.

58. Memo from Raymond Leddy to U.S. ambassador.

59. Ibid.

60. Robert Nathan, *Investment and Industrial Development in El Salvador: A Report for the Technical Cooperation Administration* (Washington, D.C.: Nathan Associates, 1961), 109.

61. Ibid., 109-110.

62. Ibid., 111.

63. Ibid.

64. Ibid., 117.

65. See Records of the Office of Middle American Affairs, 1947-1956, El Salvador File, RG-59, General Records of the State Department, National Archives, for periodic evaluations of El Salvador by the State Department. These evaluations were positive because El Salvador had implemented an industrial promotion law and had consistently supported U.S. objectives against Guatemala.

66. Philip Russell, *El Salvador in Crisis* (Austin, Tex.: Colorado River Press, 1984), 52.

67. Ibid.

68. Ibid.

69. Ibid.

70. Memo from Ernest V. Siracusa, head of Central American and Panamanian Affairs, to Miller, Assistant Secretary of State for Inter-American Affairs, March 13, 1951, Central America, Subject File, Inter-American High-

way Folder, RG-59, General Records of the State Department, National Archives.

71. Ibid.; also see memo from Assistant Secretary of State Jack McFall to Senator Chavez detailing similar rationale for building of highway, Records of the Office of Middle American Affairs, 1947-1956, Box 4, Subject File, Inter-American Highway Folder, RG-59, General Records of the State Department, National Archives.

72. Ibid.

73. Ibid.

74. Richard Feinberg, *Subsidizing Success: The Export-Import Bank in the U.S. Economy* (Cambridge: Cambridge University Press, 1982), 15.

75. Ibid., 45.

76. Ibid., 43.

77. Ibid., 44.

78. Ibid., 47.

79. Ibid., 107.

80. Thomas Zoumaras, "The Path to Pan-Americanism: Eisenhower's Foreign Economic Policy Toward Latin America," unpublished dissertation, University of Connecticut, 1987, p. 142.

81. Ibid., 142-43.

82. Ibid.

83. Ibid., 144.

84. Ibid.

85. Burton Kaufman, *Trade and Aid: Eisenhower's Foreign Economic Policy, 1953-1961*, (Baltimore: John Hopkins Univ. Press, 1982), 17-26; also see Maxfield and Nolt, 56.

86. Ibid., 30.

87. Records of the Office of Middle American Affairs, 1947-1956, Subject File, Box 4, Chronicle of Inter-Departmental Memoranda regarding Point Four program, National Archives.

88. Kaufman, 15.

89. Ibid., 16.

90. Ibid., 17.

91. Ibid., 3.

3. U.S. Intervention in Guatemala

1. NSC 144/1, "A Report to the National Security Council by the Executive Secretary on U.S. Objectives and Courses of Action with Respect to Latin America," July 23, 1953, declassified documents file, State Historical Society, University of Wisconsin-Madison.

2. National Planning Association, *The Political Economy of American Foreign Policy* (New York: Henry Holt and Co., 1955), 334.

3. Ibid., 339.

4. Ibid.

5. Ibid., 338.

6. Report by C.D. Jackson to Secretary of State John Foster Dulles, April 19, 1954, U.S. Council on Foreign Economic Policy, Dodge Series, Subject Subseries, Economic Policy 1, Box 2, Eisenhower Library.

7. Report by Walt Rostow and Max Millikan, Nov. 24, 1954, U.S. Council on Foreign Economic Policy, Dodge Series, Subject Subseries, Economic Policy 2, Box 2.

8. Ibid.

9. C.D. Jackson to Secretary of State Dulles.

10. Ibid.

11. Ibid.

12. Ibid.

13. Ibid.

14. Ibid.

15. Ibid.

16. Ibid.

17. See the U.S. Council on Foreign Economic Policy, "Fostering Free Enterprise in Underdeveloped Areas," Spring 1957, Staff Series, Eisenhower Library.

18. Eugene Staley, *The Future of Underdeveloped Countries* (New York: Council on Foreign Relations, 1954), 344-45.

19. Ibid., 346.

20. Ibid.

21. Ibid.

22. Ibid.

23. Ibid.

24. Concerning the battle over EXIM lending, the best source is Thomas Zoumaras, "The Path to Pan-Americanism: Eisenhower's Foreign Economic Policy," unpublished dissertation, University of Connecticut, 1987.

25. See the unfavorable responses to Jackson by Eisenhower and Dulles: Eisenhower to Jackson, August 16, 1954, Jackson Papers, Box 4; and Dulles to Jackson, August 24, 1954, Jackson Papers, Box 4, Eisenhower Library.

26. Report from Undersecretary of State on EXIM Bank policy in Latin America, March 29, 1955, Council on Foreign Economic Policy, 1954-1961, Dodge Series, Subject Subseries, Latin American Folder, Eisenhower Library.

27. Ibid.

28. Ibid.

29. Ibid.

30. Ibid.

31. Commission on Organization of the Executive Branch (Hoover Commission Reports) "Overseas Economi Operations" (Washington, D.C.: GPO, 1955), 51-52.

32. Ibid., 50.

33. Ibid., 54.

34. Ibid., 67.

35. Burton Kaufman, *Trade and Aid: Eisenhower's Foreign Economic Policy* (Baltimore: Johns Hopkins University Press, 1982), 48.

36. Ibid.

37. See Records of the Office of Middle American Affairs, Guatemala files, 1942-1954, Box 2, RG-59, General Records of the State Department, National Archives, for letters of correspondence between State Department officials and IRCA, United Fruit, Empressa Electrica, and J.Peter Grace on investment conditions in Guatemala.

38. Richard Immerman, *The CIA in Guatemala: The Foreign Policy of Intervention* (Austin: University of Texas Press, 1982), 73.

39. Ibid.

40. Memo from John Fischer to State Department, Nov. 16, 1954, Records of the Office of Middle American Affairs, Guatemala file, Box 2, RG-59, General Records of the State Department, National Archives.

41. Ibid.

42. Letter from W.S. Robertson, president of American and Foreign Power, to John Moors Cabot, Assistant Secretary of State for Inter-American Affairs, May 5, 1953, Records of the Office of Middle American Affairs, Guatemala file, Box 4, RG-59, General Records of the State Department, National Archives.

43. Immerman, 83.

44. Ibid.

45. Ibid.

46. Chronicle of Inter-Departmental Memoranda, May 21, 1953, Records of the Office of Middle American Affairs, 1947-1956, Subject File, Box 4, RG-59, General Records of the State Department, National Archives.

47. Ibid.

48. See letter from IRCA chairman of the board and president to U.S. Embassy, Nov. 12, 1953, Records of the Office of Middle American Affairs, Guatemala file, 1942-1954, Box 2, RG-59, General Records of the State Department, National Archives

49. Ibid.

50. Kenedon P. Seins, U.S. Department of State memorandum, May 16, 1950, Foreign Relations of United States (FRUS) 2:893; John F. Fishburn to Edward Miller, April 19, 1950, FRUS. 2:880-81; Edwin Kyle to Richard Newberger, August 4, 1947 and August 8, 1947, FRUS 8:707,711.

51. Susanne Jonas, "Anatomy of an Intervention: The U.S. Liberation of Guatemala," in *Guatemala*, ed. Susanne Jonas and David Tobis (NACLA, 1974), 60.

52. Ibid.

53. Ibid.

54. Ibid.

55. Ibid.

56. Theodore Geiger, *Communism versus Progress in Guatemala*, prepared for the NPA Committee on International Policy, (Washington, D.C.: NPA, 1953), vi-vii.

57. Ibid.

58. Jonas, 61.

59. Ibid.

60. Ibid., 81.

61. Ibid., 79.

62. Ibid.

63. Ibid., 78.

64. See memo from Thomas Mann to State Department, Oct. 30, 1954, Records of the Office of Middle American Affairs, El Salvador and Guatemala files, 1942-1954, Box 2, RG-59, General Records of the State Department, National Archives.

65. Ibid. Note that this recommendation was endorsed by President Eisenhower.

66. Jonas, 79.

67. The Eisenhower administration rejected ECLA overtures for a Central American Common Market until 1958, when President Eisenhower met with Salvadoran President Lemus to offer support for regional institutions needed to promote a common market. (See chap. 4 for details.)

68. Corporate executives insisted that U.S. government efforts to promote foreign direct investment must increase. See, for example, the letter from J. Peter Grace to Joseph M. Dodge, Special Assistant to the President, April 14, 1955, Council on Foreign Economic Series, Office of the Chairman, 1954-1961, Dodge Series, Subject Subseries, Latin American folder, Box 3, Eisenhower Library.

69. David Baldwin, *Economic Development and American Foreign Policy* (Chicago: University of Chicago Press, 1966), 216.

70. For a detailed account of this strategy, see the planning documents of the Council on Foreign Relations, *Studies of the American Interests in the War and the Peace: Economic and Financial Series*, E-A, 21:10 and 21:11 (New York: CFR, 1940-1945). Also see the National Economic and Social Planning Association (later the NPA), *War and Our Latin American Trade Policy*, Planning pamphlet no. 2, (Washington, D.C.: NESPA, 1939), 28-29. For similar views from the Committee on Economic Development, see "Foreign Investment and American Foreign Policy," Papers of Walter Salant, Point Four Program (1), Box 2, Jan. 11, 1949, and "The United States Interest in Point Four," Lloyd Papers, Point Four (1), Box 19, July 28, 1949, Truman Library.

71. In fact, internationalists made little progress in reducing tariffs on light manufactured goods in the 1950s, due in part to the item-by-item method of tariff reduction used until the Kennedy Round of the 1960s.

4. Business Welcomes Creation of Central American Common Market

1. See the Rockefeller Panel Reports, "Foreign Economic Policy for the Twentieth Century," in *Prospect for America* (New York: Doubleday and Co., Inc., 1958).

2. See the memo from Edward Galbreath to Clarence Randall, June 16, 1958, Council on Foreign Economic Policy, Randall File, Box 4, Eisenhower Library.

3. Rockefeller Panel Reports, 228.

4. Ibid., 228-29.

5. Ibid., 219.

6. Ibid.

7. Ibid.

8. Ibid., 220.

9. Ibid.

10. Ibid.

11. Ibid.

12. Ibid.

13. Ibid., 220-21.

14. Ibid., 221.

15. Ibid., 199.

16. Ibid., 230.

17. Ibid.

18. Ibid.

19. Ibid.

20. Ibid.

21. *New York Times*, Feb. 19, 1953, p. 24; and the *Encyclopedia of Associations* (Detroit, 1970), 41, cited in David Landry, "United States Interests in Central America: A Case Study of Policies Toward Economic Integration and Development from 1952 to 1968," unpublished dissertation, University of Notre Dame, 1972, 70.

22. U.S. Department of Commerce, *Investments in Central America* (Washington, 1956), 39.

23. Ibid., 41-42.

24. "Gringos Welcome: Formation of Common Market Sets Off Campaign to Attract Foreign Investment," *Business Week* Nov. 7, 1959, p. 132.

25. Gene Bylinsky, "Latin Unity? Central America Aims for Tariff-Free Area but Faces Big Obstacles," *Wall Street Journal*, Sept. 4, 1959, p. 1.

26. Memo of conversation between President Eisenhower and José Maria Lemus, March 11, 1959, Council on Foreign Economic Policy, State Department, El Salvador File, Eisenhower Library.

27. Ibid.

28. James Minotto, "Central America and the Caribbean: A Report to the U.S. Council on Foreign Economic Policy," in U.S. Council on Foreign Economic Policy, Office of the Chairman, Staff Series, Box 8, "Fostering Free Enterprise in Underdeveloped Areas," Spring 1957, Eisenhower Library.

29. Ibid.

30. See Landry, 73.

31. NSC $5613/_1$, "U.S. Policy Toward Latin America," Nov. 26, 1958.

32. Jenny Pearce, *Under the Eagle* (Boston: South End Press, 1982), 26-27.

33. Ibid., 27.

34. Secretariat for the Inter-American Economic and Social Council, *Financing of Economic Development in Latin America* (Washington, D.C.: OAS, 1958), 17.

35. Ibid.

36. Peter Dewitt, *The Inter-American Development Bank and Political Influence* (New York: Praeger Publishers, 1977), 24.

37. Ibid., 35.

38. Ibid., 36.

39. Ibid., 58.

40. Ibid.

41. Ibid., 60-61.

42. Hector Melo and Israel Yost, "Funding the Empire: Part 2, the Multinational Strategy," *North American Congress on Latin America* 4 (3): 14 (May-June 1970).

43. Susanne Jonas, "Masterminding the Mini-Market," in *Guatemala*, ed. Susanne Jonas and David Tobis (NACLA, 1974) 14.

44. Ibid.

45. Ibid., 87.

46. Ibid., 89.

47. Isaac Cohen Orantes, *Regional Integration in Central America* (Lexington, Mass.: Lexington Books-D.C. Heath, 1972), 60.

48. Jonas, 95.

49. Ibid.

50. James Cochrane, *The Politics of Regional Integration: The Central American Case* (New Orleans: Tulane University, 1969), 210.

51. Jonas 95.

52. Ibid., 94.

53. Ibid., 97.

54. Ibid.

55. For evidence of this, see the memo from Edward Galbreath to Clarence Randall (n. 2).

56. For extensive documentation of the business connections of the Eisenhower administration, see Philip Burch, *Elites in American History* (New York: Holmes and Meier, 1980), 123-67.

57. For the most concise account of the literature on the NAM and its domination by small and medium-sized U.S. businesses, see Philip Burch, "The NAM as an Interest Group," *Politics and Society*, vol. 4, no. 1 (Fall 1973): 97-130. Note that Burch, correctly I believe, rejects the claims of earlier studies of the NAM that merely assumed that its views were consistent with those of Fortune 500 firms or leading business internationalists. Burch argues that small business and "family-owned firms" with a right-wing ideology, some affiliated with the John Birch society, have been dominant in the organization at various points—including the 1950s and early 1960s.

58. Robert Baldwin, *Economic Development and American Foreign Policy: 1943-1962* (Chicago: University of Chicago Press, 1966), 146-49.

59. Thomas Ferguson and Joel Rogers, *Right Turn: The Decline of the Democrats and the Future of American Politics* (New York: Hill and Wang, 1986), 53.

60. Commission on Organization of the Executive Branch, *Hoover Com-*

mission Reports, "Overseas Economic Operations" (Washington, D.C.: GPO, 1955), 51-52.

61. For background on this, see Steve Weissman, "An Alliance for Stability" in *The Trojan Horse,* ed. Steve Weissman (Palo Alto: Ramparts Press, 1975), 75-76.

62. David Rockefeller in 1958 formed the Business Group for Latin America, which included most U.S. investors in the region. Rockefeller gave an endorsement of the Alliance for Progress in 1962 before the Economic Club of Chicago, stating, "We have made a firm commitment to Latin America for economic aid and for assistance in containing communist imperialism. I think the situation warrants substantial expenditures on both fronts on the scale proposed by President Kennedy"; cited in Jerome Levinson and Juan de Onis, *The Alliance that Lost Its Way* (Chicago: Quadrangle Books, 1970), 6-8. Also note the extensive evidence of business correspondence with administration officials on various aspects of Alliance for Progress programs, especially the following: memo from Thomas Mann to Horace Busby, Office of the White House Press Secretary, Jan. 31, 1964, National Security File, Latin America, Box 1; memo from Walt Rostow to McGeorge Bundy, Nov. 3, 1964, National Security File, Agency File, Alliance for Progress, vol. 2, Box 4; letter from David Rockefeller on behalf of the Council for Latin America (previously the Business Group for Latin America) to President Johnson, September 10, 1965, White House Central Files, Box 30, Johnson Presidential Library.

63. Cited in James Petras, *Politics and Social Structure in Latin America* (New York: Monthly Review Press, 1970), 237.

64. For evidence of this, see the Council on Foreign Relations publication *Social Change in Latin America,* (New York: Harper and Brothers, 1961), especially John Gillin, "Some Signposts for Policy," 61. Gillin gives a good overview of the affinity between the CFR and Kennedy's Alliance for Progress. In addition, see the extensive correspondence between David Rockefeller's Business Group for Latin America, the Executive Service Corps (another group of private investors), and the White House in the Lyndon Johnson Presidential Library, especially the following: memo from W.G. Bowdler to Walt Rostow, Security Council History, Box 13, 1967; and the memo from Sol Linowitz to President Johnson, March 23, 1967, from same source, indicating the extent to which David Rockefeller worked to minimize the "appearance" of private sector involvement in aid appropriations for fear of congressional opposition.

65. Petras, 237-38.

66. Ibid.

67. Ibid.

68. See the El Salvador country report, National Security Files, Agency File, Alliance for Progress, vol. 1, Box 3D, Johnson Library.

69. AID Report on El Salvador, National Security Files, Agency Files, AID, Box 3, 134, Johnson Library.

70. El Salvador Country Profile regarding AID, EXIM, and IDB projects,

National Security Files, Agency Files, Alliance for Progress, vol. 1, Box 3C, Johnson Library.

71. Report on El Salvador.

72. Ibid.

73. Ibid.

74. Ibid.

75. Marc Herold, "From Riches to 'Rags': *Finanzkapital* in El Salvador," unpublished manuscript, Whittemore School of Business and Economics, University of New Hampshire, 1980, 22-23.

76. Ibid., 22.

77. Ibid., 21.

78. Weissman.

79. See the Agency for International Development, *An Evaluation of ROCAP Activities in Marketing*, (Washington, D.C.: GPO, 1971), 10; and Joseph Pincus, *The Central American Common Market* (Washington, D.C.: ROCAP, 1962) for an earlier account of AID objectives.

80. El Salvador Report.

81. Memo to the President, July 1, 1964, National Security File, Country File, Latin America, Box 2, Johnson Library.

82. Memo to the President, July 26, 1965, National Security Files, Country File, Latin America, Box 1, Johnson Library.

5. Support for Export Promotion in Central America and the Caribbean

1. Lyndon Johnson to Secretary of State, AID administrator, Secretary of Commerce, Secretary of Agriculture, Secretary of Treasury, National Security File, National Security Action Memorandum, No. 371, Johnson Presidential Library. Also see memo from Walt Rostow to President, which states that David Rockefeller's Business Advisory Council "is deeply involved with us" in export promotion campaign.

2. See "Hope for Better Intra-CACM Relations Periled by Costa Rican Payments Move," *Business Latin America*, July 20, 1972, p. 227.

3. Ibid.

4. For a comprehensive analysis of the growth performance of Central American economies, see John Weeks, *The Economies of Central America*, (New York: Holmes and Meier, 1985), 58-71.

5. Victor Bulmer-Thomas, "Can Regional Import-Substitution and Export-Led Growth Be Combined," in *Central America*, ed. George Irvin and Stuart Holland, 68-69.

6. Memo from Johnson to Secretary of State.

7. Alfredo Guerra-Borges, "Industrial Development in Central America, 1960-1980: Issues of Debate," ibid., 53.

8. See "Firestone Marketing Push in CACM Permits Continued Full Production," *Business Latin America*, March 9, 1972, and "Kimberly-Clark's El Salvador Plant a Vote of Confidence in CACM's Future," ibid., Jan. 7, 1971.

9. See chap. 5 for documentation, especially the Rockefeller Panel Re-

ports, "Foreign Economic Policy for the Twentieth Century" in *Prospect for America*, (New York: Doubleday and Co., Inc., 1958).

10. See Marc Herold, "From Riches to 'Rags': *Finanzkapital* in El Salvador, 1900-1980," unpublished manuscript, Whitmore School of Business and Economics, University of New Hampshire, 1980.

11. Allan Nairn, "Guatemala," *Multinational Monitor*, May 1981, p. 13.

12. Herold, p. 23.

13. Norma Stoltz Chinchilla and Nora Hamilton, "Prelude to Revolution: U.S. Investment in Central America," in *The Politics of Intervention*, ed. Roger Burbach and Patricia Flynn New York: Monthy Review Press, 1984, 234.

14. Ibid.

15. See Johnson memo to Secretary of State.

16. See *Business Latin America*; also see *BLA*, Jan. 30, 1969, and Sept. 10, 1970, p. 291.

17. Memo from the Vice-President to the President, "The Food Situation in Latin America," April 6, 1966, National Security File, Country File, Latin America, 1963-66, Box 5, Johnson Presidential Library.

18. Ibid.

19. "El Salvador First in CACM to Offer Incentives for Exports Outside Region," *Business Latin America*, March 25, 1971, p. 96.

20. Ibid.

21. Ibid.

22. Ibid.

23. Herold, p. 24.

24. For evidence of this, see U.S. State Department, *Background Notes: Guatemala* (Washington, D.C.: Superintendent of Documents, July 1981), p. 1, where former Overseas Private Investment Corporation President Bruce Llewellyn argues to Congress that the AVX assembly plant in El Salvador allows the company to compete better against Japanese manufacturers.

25. Herold, p. 24.

26. Tom Barry, Beth Wood, and Deb Preusch, *The Other Side of Paradise* (New York: Grove Press, Inc., 1988), 59.

27. Ibid., 67-70.

28. Ibid., 25-26.

29. Chinchilla and Hamilton, 227.

30. Barry et al., 25.

31. See Susanne Jonas, "The New Hard Line," in Guatemala, ed. Susanne Jonas and David Tobis (New York: NACLA, 1974), p. 109, for a discussion of the business group Partners of the Alliance, which was instrumental in bringing together elected officials and U.S. businessmen interested in export ventures.

32. Chinchilla and Hamilton, 228.

33. Memo from the President to the Secretary of State.

34. Richard Feinberg, *Subsidizing Success: The Export-Import Bank in the U.S. Economy* (New York: Cambridge University Press, 1982), 44.

35. Barry et al., 50.

36. Roger Burbach and Marc Herold, "The U.S. Economic Stake in Central America and the Caribbean," in *The Politics of Intervention*, 198-99. New York: Monthly Review Press, 1984.

37. Herold.

38. Richard Feinberg, *The Intemperate Zone: The Third World Challenge to U.S. Foreign Policy* (New York: W.W. Norton and Company, 1983), 94-95.

39. Burbach and Herold, 199-200.

40. Feinberg, 84-85.

41. Ibid., 87-88.

42. Ibid., 88.

43. For background on the Council, see Lars Schoultz, *Human Rights and United States Policy Toward Latin America* (Princeton, N.J.: Princeton University Press, 1981), 66-72.

44. Rostow memo to the President.

45. See the reports from the Advisory Panel, Activities of the Bureau of Inter-American Affairs (a business-government panel), National Security File, Country File, Latin America, 1966-1969, Box 5, Johnson Library.

46. Thomas Mann to the President regarding the working relationship with the Business Group for Latin America, National Security File, Country File, Latin America, Box 2, Vol. 3, $^1/_{65}$-$^6/_{65}$, Johnson Library.

47. Jonas.

48. Tom Barry and Deb Preusch, *The Central America Fact Book*, (Albuquerque, N.M.: Resource Center, 1986), 155-56.

49. Burbach and Herold, 193.

50. As an indication of the commitment to industries still producing for the CACM, see the memo to the President from the Bureau of the Budget regarding the $30 million loan to the Central American Bank's Fund for Economic Integration, July 3, 1968, National Security File, Country File, Latin America, Box 5.

51. U.S. AID mission in Guatemala, memo on "Export Development," July 16, 1970.

52. See the memo to the President from the Bureau of the Budget.

53. Jonas.

54. For an elaboration of the policies of the Nixon administration regarding U.S. aid to Latin America, see "Outlook for U.S. Aid, Trade Policies Promises Few Sweeteners for Latins," *Business Latin America*, April 29, 1971, p. 134.

55. Jonas, 109.

56. Ibid.

57. Feinberg, 45.

58. Ibid.

59. Ibid.

60. "Export-Import Bank, 50 Firms Set Boost in Credit Insurance," *Wall Street Journal*, April 21, 1970, p. 37; also see "Eximbank Revises Insuring Program," *New York Times*, April 21, 1970, p. 4C.

61. For details on the shift in EXIM lending strategies, see the memo

from Peter Flanigan, Assistant to the President, to Henry Kearns, Director of EXIM, April 30, 1970, and related documents at the Nixon Project, EX, FO 4-2 (1969-70), Box 46.

62. Tom Barry, Beth Wood, and Deb Preusch, *Dollars and Dictators: A Guide to Central America* (Albuquerque, N.M.: The Resource Center, 1983), 26.

63. Ibid.

64. Ibid., 103.

65. Ibid., 102-03.

66. Ibid.

67. Agency for International Development, "An Evaluation of ROCAP Activities in Marketing" (Washington, D.C.: GPO, 1971), 72.

68. Ibid.

69. Ibid., 71-72.

70. Jonas, 111.

71. Agency for International Development 102-103.

6. The Shift Toward Economic Stabilization and More Military Aid

1. This model is taken from the framework provided by Thomas Ferguson, "From Normalcy to New Deal: Industrial Structure, Party Competition, and American Public Policy in the Great Depression," *International Organization* 38, 1, (Winter 1984). Capital- and labor-intensive firms are defined by "wages as a percent of value-added in production," with labor-intensive firms being more dependent on low-wage labor for a significant percentage of their costs. Using this framework, commercial banks and petroleum firms are the most capital-intensive firms active in Central America. They have also been the most frequent opponents of military "solutions" to the region.

2. James Kurth, "The United States and Central America: Hegemony in Historical and Comparative Perspective," in *Central America: International Dimensions of the Crisis*, ed. Richard Feinberg. (New York: Holmes and Meier, 1982), 54.

3. Morris Morley and James Petras, "Sacrificing Dictators to Preserve the State: Permanent and Transitory Interests in U.S. Foreign Policy," in *Rethinking Marxism*, vol. 3, (Fall-Winter 1990): 139. The quotes are from Department of State Telegram, Secret State 153522, Secretary of State to All American Republic Diplomatic Posts, 13 June 1979, subject: "OAS Action on Nicaragua," Declassified Freedom of Information Act; and Secretary of State Cyrus Vance in U.S. Congress, House, Committee on Foreign Affairs, Sub-Committee on Inter-American Affairs, United States Policy Toward Nicaragua, 96th Cong., 1st sess., June 21 and 26, 1979, 72.

4. Much of this analysis relies on Susanne Jonas, "The New Cold War and the Nicaraguan Revolution: The Case of U.S. Aid to Nicaragua," in *Revolution and Intervention in Central America*, ed. Susanne Jonas and Marlene Dixon (San Francisco: Synthesis Publications, 1981), 219-236.

5. Ibid.

6. Holly Sklar, *Washington's War on Nicaragua* (Boston: South End Press, 1988), 62.

7. About fifty-four foreign corporations maintained operations in Nicaragua after the 1979 revolution. These firms included Xerox Corporation, Transamerica Airlines, American Life Insurance, Chevron Corporation, General Mills, and others mentioned in the body of the text. By all accounts, most of these firms maintained acceptable, if not good, relations with the Sandinista government. For information on the generally favorable relations between U.S. capital-intensive firms and the Sandinistas, see the Nicaragua File, Overseas Private Investment Corporation Library, Washington, D.C.

8. *Miami Report*, (University of Miami: Caribbean Review, 1984). Note that the report was endorsed by Juan Yanes, president, Esso Caribbean and Central America, and by Dennis Nason, president, Florida International Bankers Association, as well as Esteban A Ferrer, partner of Shutts and Bowen; president-elect, International Center of Florida; and president of the Miami Chapter of the Council of the Americas.

9. For a discussion of these issues, see Richard Feinberg, *The Intemperate Zone* (New York: W.W. Norton and Co., 1983), 90-91.

10. Tom Barry and Deb Preusch, *The Central America Fact Book*, (New York: Grove Press, 1986), 296.

11. Ibid., 289.

12. A split emerged within the group Caribbean/Central American Action between capital-intensive and labor-intensive firms over U.S. policy toward Central America. Capital-intensive firms, including those cited in the text, generally were skeptical of, if not openly opposed, to the Reagan administration's policies. As a result, CCAA was unable to take a stand on increased military aid to the region. This information is based on documents obtained from the El Salvador file, Overseas Private Investment Corporation Library; and from an interview with Sergio Alvarez, assistant director, investment promotion, Caribbean/Central American Action. The Salvador file reveals that commercial banks and the oil firm Esso were concerned that U.S. policies would promote further instability. Also see Miami Report, 1984.

13. On U.S. investments and political influence in Guatemala, see Allan Nairn, "Guatemala" in *Multinational Monitor*, May 1981, pp. 12-14.

14. The association is on record as supporting increased military aid to the Nicaraguan contras and to the Guatemalan and Salvadoran governments. See Sklar, 115. Also see Lars Schoultz, *Human Rights and United States Policy Toward Latin America* (Princeton N.J.: Princeton University Press, 1981), 73.

15. For extensive background on the committee, see Jerry Sanders, *Peddlers of Crisis* (Boston: South End Press, 1983. For a list of committee members in the Reagan administration, see pp. 287-89.

16. The Committee of Santa Fe, part of the Council for Inter-American Security is one good example of an ideologically motivated group. See their report, "A New Inter-American Policy for the Eighties," (Washington, D.C.: Council for Inter-American Security, 1980).

17. Carlos Vilas, *State, Class and Ethnicity in Nicaragua* (Boulder, Colo.: Lynne Rienner Publishers, 1989), 44.

18. Ibid.

19. Ibid., 44-45.

20. Ibid.

21. Ibid., 45.

22. Ibid., 76-77.

23. Ibid., 48-49.

24. Ibid., 49.

25. Ibid., 48.

26. Ibid., 110.

27. Ibid., 108-9.

28. Ibid., 110.

29. Ibid.

30. Robert Holden, "Corporate Officials Embrace Latin Dictators at Private Chamber of Commerce Session," *Multinational Monitor* (June 1982): 1-3. Also see the report on an ACCLA position paper advocating more U.S. military training and equipment for allies in Central America, *Business Latin America*, April 13, 1983, p. 115.

31. *Business Latin America*, April 13, 1983, p. 115.

32. Ibid.

33. For a detailed account of the sourcing strategy, see the Business International Corporation, *Improving International Competitiveness Through Sourcing in Latin America* (New York: BIC, 1989).

34. Allan Nairn, "Guatemala," *Multinational Monitor*, May 1981, pp. 12-14. Note that Bank of America also supported these death squads and advocated military aid to Guatemala. This differed from the bank's position in El Salvador and Nicaragua, where bank officials urged economic solutions. The primary reason for the difference was that the bank operated as an investment bank in Guatemala, with loans extended to U.S. manufacturing and agribusiness firms in the country. Thus the bank had a direct interest in supporting security forces, which controlled labor unrest in these industries. In El Salvador and Nicaragua, on the other hand, the bank's loans were primarily to the state sector or to capital-intensive firms.

35. Kenichi Ohmae, *Triad Power: The Coming Shape of Global Competition* (New York: Free Press, 1985).

36. BIC, pp. 2-4.

37. Ibid., 14-15.

38. The CCAA (now called the Caribbean Latin American Action) has published several articles on sourcing strategies to assist member firms, including one in its bulletin *Caribbean Action* 7 (2): (January 1992). This issue highlights the effectiveness of sourcing production in Puerto Rico, the Dominican Republic, and Costa Rica for a number of U.S. firms, including Westinghouse, Johnson and Johnson, Milton Shoe Company, Schering Plough, Sara Lee Corporation, General Electric and Suttle, Inc.

39. There is an extensive body of literature that documents the connections of the Committee on the Present Danger to the Reagan administration. For a recent overview, see Simon Dalby, *Creating the Second Cold War* (London: Pinter Publishers, 1990). Also see the Committee on the Present Danger, *Alerting America: The Papers of the Committee on the Present Danger* (Washington, D.C.: CPD, 1984).

40. "ACCLA Position Paper," *Business Latin America*, April 13, 1983, p. 115.

41. Interview with Sergio Alvarez, assistant director, investment promotion, Caribbean/Central American Action, July 25, 1990.

42. There are numerous legislative histories of the CBI compiled by the CCAA. For a concise statement of corporate support for the initiative, see David Rockefeller, "Reaffirming the U.S. Commitment to the Caribbean Basin," statement to the Subcommittee on Trade of the Committee on Ways and Means, U.S. House of Representatives, Hearings on Legislation to Improve the Caribbean Basin Initiative, March 28, 1988, CCAA Files. Also see issues of the CCAA newsletter throughout the 1980s for a history of its lobbying for the CBI. Note that the CCAA was created in 1979 with the explicit purpose of pressuring political officials for the passage of the CBI well before it became a Reagan administration proposal.

43. For an analysis of these provisions, see Emilio Pantojas-Garcia, "The U.S. Caribbean Basin Initiative and the Puerto Rican Experience," *Latin American Perspectives* 12 (Fall 1985): 105-28. Also see Hilbourne Watson, "Caribbean Basin Initiative and Caribbean Development," *Contemporary Marxism* no. 10: 1-37. For analyses of the internationalization of capital in the 1970s that provided useful information for this study, see James Cypher, "The Crisis and Restructuring of Capital in the Periphery," *Research in Political Economy* vol. 2, 1988, especially pp. 65-78; Martin Landsberg, "Export-led Industrialization in the Third World: Manufacturing Imperialism," *Review of Radical Political Economics* 11:4 (Winter 1979); and Paul Zarembka, "Accumulation of Capital in the Periphery," in *Research in Political Economy*, vol. 2, pp. 99-140.

44. Pantojas-Garcia, 107-8.

45. Ibid., 114.

46. Ibid.

47. Frederick Brooks, "Next Step for CBI—Get Rid of Textile Quotas," *Caribbean Action*, Summer 1985, p. 6.

7. The Business Conflict Model

1. Susanne Jonas, "The New Cold War and the Nicaraguan Revolution: The Case of U.S. Aid to Nicaragua," in *Revolution and Intervention in Central America*, ed. Susanne Jonas and Marlene Dixon (San Francisco: Synthesis Publications, 1981), 224.

2. David Gibbs applied his variant of the model to U.S. intervention in Zaire in *The Political Economy of Third World Intervention* (Chicago: University

of Chicago Press, 1991). For the best detailed study of business influence on U.S. policy toward Asia during the first cold war, see Bruce Cumings, ed., *Child of Conflict* (Seattle: University of Washington Press, 1983), especially Cumings's introductory essay.

3. See Michael Hogan, *The Marshall Plan* (Cambridge: Cambridge University Press, 1985).

Bibliography

Agency for International Development. *An Evaluation of ROCAP Activities in Marketing.* Washington: GPO, 1971.

Baldwin, David. *Economic Development and American Foreign Policy.* Chicago: University of Chicago Press, 1966.

Baldwin, Robert. *The Political Economy of U.S. Import Policy.* Cambridge: MIT Press, 1985.

Barry, Tom, and Deb Preusch. *The Central America Fact Book.* Albuquerque, N.M.: Resource Center, 1986.

―――. *The Soft War.* New York: Grove Press, 1988.

Barry, Tom, Beth Wood, and Deb Preusch. *Dollars and Dictators.* Albuquerque, N.M.: Resource Center, 1983.

―――. *The Other Side of Paradise.* New York: Grove Press, 1988.

Bauer, Raymond, Itheal de Sola Pool, and Lewis Anthony Dexter. *American Business and Public Policy.* Chicago: Aldine and Atherton, 1972.

Blaiser, Cole. *The Hovering Giant.* Pittsburgh: University of Pittsburgh Press, 1976.

Block, Fred. *The Origins of International Economic Disorder.* Berkeley: University of California Press, 1977.

―――. "The Ruling Class Does Not Rule." *Socialist Revolution* 7 (3): 1977.

Brownstein, Ronald, and Nina Easton. *Reagan's Ruling Class.* New York: Pantheon Books, 1982.

Bulmer-Thomas, Victor. "Can Regional Import-Substitution and Export-led Growth Be Combined?" In *Central America,* ed. George Irvin and Stuart Holland. Boulder, Colo.: Westview Press, 1989.

Burbach, Roger, and Marc Herold. "The U.S. Economic Stake in Central America and the Caribbean." In *The Politics of Intervention,* ed. Roger Burbach and Patricia Flynn. New York: Monthly Review Press, 1984.

Burch, Philip. *Elites in American History.* New York: Holmes and Meier, 1980.

―――. "The NAM as an Interest Group." *Politics and Society,* Fall 1983, pp. 97-130.

Business International Corporation. *Improving International Competitiveness through Sourcing in Latin America*. New York: BIC, 1989.

Bylinsky, Gene. "Latin Unity? Central America Airs for Tariff-Free Area but Faces Big Obstacles." *Wall Street Journal*, Sept. 4, 1959.

Cehelsky, Maria. "Guatemala's Frustrated Revolution: The Liberation of 1954." M.A. thesis, Columbia University, 1967.

"Central America Closes Ranks." *Business Week*, March 16, 1963.

Chinchilla, Norma Stoltz, and Nora Hamilton. "Prelude to Revolution: U.S. Investment in Central America." In *The Politics of Intervention*, ed. Roger Burbach and Patricia Flynn. New York: Monthly Review Press, 1984.

Cochrane, James. *The Politics of Regional Integration: The Central American Case*. New Orleans: Tulane University, 1969.

———. "U.S. Attitudes toward Central American Economic Integration." *Inter-American Affairs*, Autumn 1964, pp. 73-91.

Cohen, Stephen. *The Making of United States International Economic Policy*. New York: Praeger Publishers, 1988.

Commission on the Organization of the Executive Branch. (Hoover Commission Reports.) "Overseas Economic Operations." Washington: GPO, 1955.

Committee for Economic Development. *Economic Development Abroad and the Role of American Foreign Investment*. New York: CED, 1956.

———. *Reports 1 and 2*. New York: CED, 1956.

Committee of Santa Fe. "A New Inter-American Policy for the Eighties." Washington, D.C.: Council for Inter-American Security: 1980.

Council on Foreign Relations. *Social Change in Latin America*. New York: Harper and Brothers, 1961.

Council on Foreign Relations. *Studies of American Interests in the War and the Peace, Economic and Financial Series*. New York: CFR, 1940-45.

Council on Foreign Relations. *The War and Peace Studies of the Council on Foreign Relations*. New York: CFR, 1939-45.

Cuadrado, J.A. "Nicaragua: Despite Reagan's Aid Cutoff, Bankers Play Ball with Sandinistas." *Multinational Monitor*, May 1981, pp. 22-24.

Cumings, Bruce, ed. *Child of Conflict*. Seattle: University of Washington Press, 1983.

Cypher, James M. "The Crisis and Restructuring of Capital in the Periphery." *Research in Political Economy*, vol. 2 (1988): 65-78.

Destler, I.M. and John S. Odell. *Anti-Protection: Changing Forces in United States Trade Politics*. Washington: Institute for International Economics, 1987.

DeWitt, Peter. *The Inter-American Development Bank and Political Influence*. New York: Praeger Publishers, 1977.

Domhoff, William. "Who Made American Foreign Policy: 1945-1963." In *Corporations and the Cold War*, ed. David Horowitz. New York: Monthly Review Press, 1969.

Domhoff, William. *The Higher Circles*. New York: Vintage Books, 1970.

Domhoff, William. *The Power Elite and the State*. New York: Walter de Gruyter, 1990.

"El Salvador First in CACM to Offer Incentives for Exports Outside Region." *Business Latin America*, March 25, 1971.

Evans, John W. *The Kennedy Round in American Trade Policy: The Twilight of the GATT*. Cambridge: Harvard University Press, 1971.

Feinberg, Richard. *The Intemperate Zone: The Third World Challenge to U.S. Foreign Policy*. New York: W.W. Norton and Company, 1983.

——. *Subsidizing Success: The Export-Import Bank in the U.S. Economy*. Cambridge: Cambridge University Press, 1982.

Ferguson, Thomas. "Party Realignment and the American Industrial Structure: The Investment Theory of Political Parties in Historical Perspective," In *Research in Political Economy* 6, ed. Paul Zarembka. London: JAI Press, 1983.

Ferguson, Thomas, and Joel Rogers. *Right Turn: The Decline of the Democrats and the Future of American Politics*. New York: Hill and Wang, 1986.

Ferguson, Thomas. "From Normalcy to New Deal: Industrial Structure, Party Competition, and American Public Policy in the Great Depression." *International Organization* 38 (Winter 1984): 41-93.

"Firestone Marketing Push in CACM Permits Continued Full Production." *Business Latin America*, March 9, 1972.

Frieden, Jeffrey. *Debt, Development and Democracy*. Princeton N.J.: Princeton University Press, 1991.

——. "Sectoral Conflict and U.S. Foreign Economic Policy." In *The State and American Foreign Economic Policy*, ed. John Ikenberry, David Lake, and Michael Mastanduno. Ithaca: Cornell University Press, 1989.

Geiger, Theodore. *Communism versus Progress in Guatemala*. Washington, D.C.: NPA, 1953.

Gibbs, David. *The Political Economy of Third World Intervention*. Chicago: University of Chicago Press, 1991.

Gilpin, Robert. *U.S. Power and the Multinational Corporation*. New York: Basic Books, 1975.

Gold, David, Clarence Lo, and Eric Olin Wright, "Recent Developments in the Marxist Theory of the Capitalist State." *Monthly Review* 27, no. 5 (1975): 29-43.

Gourevitch, Peter. *Politics in Hard Times*. Ithaca: Cornell University Press, 1986.

——. "The Second Image Reversed," *International Organization* 32 (Autumn 1978): pp. 881-912.

Gowa, Joanne. "Subsidizing American Corporate Expansion Abroad: Pitfalls in the Analysis of Public and Private Power." *World Politics* 37: (1985): 180-203.

Green, David. *The Containment of Latin America*. Chicago: Quadrangle Books, 1971.

Grieco, Joseph. *Cooperation Among Nations*. Ithaca: Cornell University Press, 1990.

"Gringos Welcome: Formation of Common Market Sets Off Campaign to Attract Foreign Investment." *Business Week*, Nov. 7, 1959, p. 132.

Guerra-Borges, Alfredo. "Industrial Development in Central America, 1960-1980: Issues of Debate." In *Central America*, ed. George Irvin and Stuart Holland. Boulder, Colo.: Westview Press, 1989.

Haggard, Stephen. "The Institutional Foundations of Hegemony: Explaining the Reciprocal Trade Agreements Act of 1934." In *The State and American Foreign Economic Policy*, ed. G. John Ikenberry, David A. Lake, and Michael Mastanduno. Ithaca: Cornell University Press, 1988.

Hardin, Russell. *Collective Action*. Baltimore: Johns Hopkins University Press, 1982.

Herold, Marc. "From Riches to Rags: Finanzkapital in El Salvador, 1900-1980," Unpublished manuscript, University of New Hampshire, Feb. 27, 1980.

Hogan, Michael. *The Marshall Plan*. Cambridge: Cambridge University Press, 1985.

Holden, Robert. "Corporate Officials Embrace Latin Dictators at Private Chamber of Commerce Session." *Multinational Monitor* (June 1982): 1-3.

"Hope for Better Intra-CACM Relations Periled by Costa Rican Payments Move." *Business Latin America*, July 20, 1972, p. 727.

Ikenberry, G. John, David A. Lake, and Michael Mastanduno. "Introduction: Approaches to Explaining American Foreign Economic Policy." In *The State and American Foreign Economic Policy*, ed. Ikenberry, Lake, Mastanduno. Ithaca: Cornell University Press, 1988.

Immerman, Richard. *The CIA in Guatemala: The Foreign Policy of Intervention*. Austin: University of Texas Press, 1982.

International Development Advisory Board. *Partners in Progress: A Report to the President*. Washington, D.C.: GPO, March 1951.

Jonas, Susanne. "The Democracy Which Gave Way: The Guatemala Revolution of 1944-1954." In *Guatemala*, ed. Susanne Jonas and David Tobis, 44-54. New York: NACLA, 1974.

Jonas, Susanne. "Masterminding the Mini-Market." In *Guatemala*, ed. Susanne Jonas and David Tobis pp. 86-103. NACLA, 1974.

———. "The New Cold War and the Nicaraguan Revolution: The Case of U.S. Aid to Nicaragua." In *Revolution and Intervention in Central America*, ed. Susanne Jonas and Marlene Dixon, pp. 219-236. San Francisco: Synthesis Publications, 1981.

Joseph, Paul. *Cracks in the Empire: State Politics in the Vietnam War*. New York: Columbia University Press, 1987.

Kaufman, Burton. *Trade and Aid: Eisenhower's Foreign Economic Policy, 1953-1961*. Baltimore: John Hopkins University Press, 1982.

Krasner, Stephen. *Defending the National Interest*. Princeton: Princeton University Press, 1978.

Kurth, James. "The Political Consequences of the Product Cycle," *International Organization* 33 (Winter 1979): 1-34.

Kurth, James. "The United States and Central America: Hegemony in Historical and Comparative Perspective." In *Central America: International Dimensions of the Crisis*, ed. Richard Feinberg. New York: Holmes and Meier, 1982.

Landry, David. "United States Interests in Central America: A Case Study of Policies toward Economic Integration and Development from 1952 to 1968." Unpublished dissertation, University of Notre Dame, 1972.

Lake, David A. *Power, Protection and Free Trade: International Sources of U.S. Commercial Strategy 1887-1939*. Ithaca: Cornell University Press, 1988.

———. "The State and American Trade Strategy in the Pre-hegemonic Era." in *The State and American Foreign Economic Policy*, eds. David Lake, G. John Ikenberry and Michael Mastanduno. Ithaca: Cornell University Press, 1988.

———. "Toward a Realist Theory of State Action." *International Studies Quarterly* 33, 4 (Dec. 1989): 457-74.

Landsberg, Martin. "Export-led Industrialization in the Third World: Manufacturing Imperialism." *Review of Radical Political Economics* 11 (Winter 1979): 4.

Levinson, Jerome, and Juan de Onis. *The Alliance That Lost Its Way*, Chicago: Quadrangle Books, 1972.

Lindbloom, Charles. *Politics and Markets*. New York: Basic Books, 1977.

Lowenthal, Abraham, *The Dominican Intervention*. Cambridge: Harvard University Press, 1972.

Lowenthal, Abraham. "United States Policy toward Latin America: Liberal, Radical and Bureaucratic Perspectives." *Latin American Research Review* 8, no. 3 (1973):?

McClintock, Michael. *The American Connection. Vol. 3, State Terror and Popular Resistance in El Salvador*. London: Zed Books Ltd., 1985.

McCormick, Tom. *America's Half-Century: United States Foreign Policy in the Cold War*. Baltimore and London: Johns Hopkins Press, 1989.

McLellan, David, and Charles Woodhouse. "The Business Elite and Foreign Policy." *Western Political Quarterly* 13 (March 1960): 172-90.

McNall, Scott, Rhonda Levine, and Rick Fantasia, *Bringing Class Back In*. Boulder, Colo.: Westview Press, 1991.

Major, Elkanah I. "The Caribbean Basin Initiative: An Analysis of United States Policy toward Central America and the Caribbean in the 1980s." Unpublished dissertation, Atlantic University, 1990.

Mallalieu, William C. *British Reconstruction and American Policy*. New York: Scarecrow Press, 1956.

Maxfield, Sylvia, and James Nolt, "Protectionism and the Internationalization of Capital: U.S. Sponsorship of Import Substitution Industrialization in the Philippines, Turkey and Argentina." *International Studies Quarterly* 34 (March): 49-81.

Melo, Hector, and Israel Yost. "Funding the Empire: Part 2, The Multinational Strategy," *North American Congress on Latin America* 4, 3, (May-June 1970).

The Miami Report: Recommendations on United States Policy Toward Latin America and the Caribbean. Miami: University of Miami, 1983.

Milbrath, Lester. "Interest Groups and Foreign Policy." In *Domestic Sources of Foreign Policy*, ed. James N. Rosenau. New York: Free Press, 1967.

Milner, Helen. *Resisting Protectionism: Global Industries and the Politics of International Trade*. Princeton, N.J.: Princeton University Press, 1988.

Nathan, Robert. *Investment and Industrial Development in El Salvador: A Report for the Technical Cooperation Administration*. Washington: Nathan Associates, 1961.

Moreno, Dario. *U.S. Policy in Central America: The Endless Debate*. Miami: Florida International University Press, 1990.

Morley, Morris. *Imperial State and Revolution: The United States and Cuba, 1952-1986*. Cambridge: Cambridge University Press, 1987.

Morley, Morris, and James Petras. "Sacrificing Dictators to Save the State: Permanent and Transitory Interests in U.S. Foreign Policy" in *Rethinking Marxism* 3 (3-4): 127-148 (Fall-Winter 1990).

Nairn, Allan. "Bank of America Asked to Explain Its Support for Guatemalan Death Squads" in *Multinational Monitor* (March 1982): 1-3.

Nairn, Allan. "Guatemala" in *Multinational Monitor*, May 1981, pp. 12-14.

National Foreign Trade Council. *Foreign Trade Reconstruction Studies No. 2*. New York: NFTC, 1943.

National Industrial Conference Board. *Economic Background for Postwar Reconstruction*. New York: NICB, 1943.

National Planning Association. *International Development Loans*. Planning pamphlets no. 15. Washington, D.C.: NPA, 1939.

———. "Promoting United States Investment Abroad." In *Planning Pamphlet on Foreign Economic Policy*. Washington, D.C.: NPA, October 1955.

———. *War and Our Latin American Trade Policy*. Planning pamphlets no. 2. New York: NFTC, 1943.

Ogene, F. Chidozie. *Interest Groups and the Shaping of Foreign Policy*. New York: St. Martin's Press, 1983.

Ohmae, Kenichi. *Triad Power: The Coming Shape of Global Competition*. New York: Free Press, 1985.

Olson, Mancur. *The Logic of Collective Action: Public Goods and the Theory of Groups*. Cambridge: Harvard University Press, 1965.

Orantes, Isaac Cohen. *Regional Integration in Central America*. Lexington, Mass.: Lexington Books-D.C. Heath, 1972.

"Outlook for U.S. Aid, Trade Policies Promises Few Sweeteners for Latins." *Business Latin America*, April 29, 1971, p. 134.

Pantojas-Garcia, Emilio. "The U.S. Caribbean Basin Initiative and the Puerto Rican Experience." *Latin American Perspectives* 12, (Fall 1985): 105-28.

Pastor, Robert. *Congress and the Politics of U.S. Foreign Economic Policy, 1929-1976*. Berkeley: University of California Press, 1988.

Pearce, Jenny. *Under the Eagle*. Boston: South End Press, 1982.

Petras, James. *Politics and Social Structure in Latin America*. New York: Monthly Review Press, 1970.

Petras, James, H. Michael Erisman and Charles Mills, "The Monroe Doctrine and U.S. Hegemony in Latin America." In *Latin America: From Dependence to Revolution*, ed. James Petras. New York: John Wiley and sons, Inc., 1973.

Petras, James, and Morris Morley. "Economic Expansion, Political Crisis and U.S. Policy in Central America." In *Revolution and Intervention in Central America*, ed. Susanne Jonas and Marlene Dixon (San Francisco: Synthesis, 1981), pp. 189-218.

———. *U.S. Hegemony Under Siege*. New York: Verso Press, 1990.

Pincus, Joseph. *The Central American Common Market*. Washington, D.C.: ROCAP, 1962.

Poulantzas, Nicos. *Political Power and Social Classes*. London: New Left Books, 1969.

"A Preview of the United States Position at the Rio Conference" *Department of State Bulletin* 31, Nov. 1954, p. 688.

The Rockefeller Panel Reports. "Foreign Economic Policy for the Twentieth Century." In *Prospect for America*. New York: Doubleday and Co., 1958.

Rogers, Joel, and Thomas Ferguson, eds. *The Hidden Election*. (New York: Pantheon, 1981).

Russell, Philip. *El Salvador in Crisis*. Austin, Tex.: Colorado River Press, 1984.

Sanders, Jerry. *Peddlers of Crisis*. Boston: South End Press, 1983.

Schoultz, Lars. *Human Rights and United States Policy Toward Latin America*. Princeton, N.J.: Princeton University Press, 1981.

Schulz, Donald, and Douglas A. Graham, eds. *Revolution and Counterrevolution in Central America and the Caribbean*. Boulder, Colo.: Westview Press, 1984.

Secretariat for the Inter-American Economic and Social Council. *Financing of Economic Development in Latin America*. Washington, D.C.: OAS, 1958.

Shoup, Laurence, and William Minter. *Imperial Brain Trust*. New York: Monthly Review Press, 1977.

Sklar, Holly. *Washington's War on Nicaragua*. Boston: South End Press, 1988.

Skocpol, Theda, "Bringing the State Back In." In *Bringing the State Back In*, ed. Peter Evans, Dietrich B. Rueschemeyer, and Theda Skocpol. London: Cambridge University Press, 1985.

Staley, Eugene. *The Future of Underdeveloped Countries*. New York: Council on Foreign Relations, 1954.

U.S. Department of Commerce. *Investments in Central America*. Washington, D.C.: 1956.

U.S. Department of State. "Background Notes: Guatemala" Washington, D.C.: Superintendent of Documents, July 1981.

Vilas, Carlos. *State, Class and Ethnicity in Nicaragua* Boulder, Colo.: Lynne Rienner Publishers, 1989.

Vogel, David. "The New Political Science of Corporate Power," *Public Interest* no. 87 (1987): 63-64.

Walton, Richard. *Cold War and Counter-Revolution: The Foreign Policy of John F. Kennedy*. Baltimore: Pelican Books, 1973.

Watson, Hilbourne. "Caribbean Basin Initiative and Caribbean Development" *Contemporary Marxism* 10 (1985): 1-37.

Weeks, John. *The Economies of Central America*. New York: Holmes and Meier, 1985.

Weissman, Steve. "The Alliance for Stability." In *The Trojan Horse*. Palo Alto, Calif.: Ramparts Press, 1975.

Wilson, Joan Hoff. *American Business and Foreign Policy*. Lexington: University Press of Kentucky, 1971.

Wood, Robert. *From Marshall Plan to Debt Crisis*. Berkeley: University of California Press, 1986.

The World Bank. *The World Bank Group in the Americas*. Washington, D.C.: GPO, 1972.

Zarembka, Paul. "Accumulation of Capital in the Periphery." *Research in Political Economy*, vol. 2 (1979): 99-140.

Zoumaras, Thomas. "The Path to Pan-Americanism: Eisenhower's Foreign Economic Policy Toward Latin America." Ph.D. dissertation, University of Connecticut, 1987.

U.S. Government: Archival Sources

National Archives of the United States. (Washington, D.C.) General Records of the Department of State. Record Group 59.

Records of the United States Senate, Committee on Foreign Relations. Record Group 46.

Presidential Libraries

The Harry S. Truman Presidential Library. Independence, Mo.
The Dwight D. Eisenhower Presidential Library. Abilene, Kans.
The Lyndon B. Johnson Presidential Library. Austin, Texas.
The Nixon Project. Alexandria, Va.

Index

ELI (export-led industrialization), 22,
23, 46, 64, 65, 71, 139
elitist models, 2
El Salvador: and Agency for International Development (AID), 84,
85-88; and Caribbean Basin Initiative (CBI), 130; and Central American Common Market (CACM), 70,
77, 86, 87, 90, 94, 158 n 67; export
promotion in, 93, 95, 96, 97, 99,
102, 103, 106, 124; government assistance for U.S. business in, 95,
96, 121; Industrial Promotion Law
of 1952, 37-38, 154 n 65; Inter-
American Highway project in, 29,
39-40; liberal vs. labor-intensive
business and policy on, 10, 15-16;
military aid to, in 1970s-80s, 16,
110, 116, 117, 120, 121, 125, 145,
165 n 14; and Point Four program,
35-39, 151 n 17; in Tripartite Agreement, 77; World Bank lending programs in, descsribed, 32
Empressa Electric, 56, 57-58, 62
enclave economy, 117-18
Esso, 64
Esso Caribbean and Central America,
165 n 8
Esso Standard Oil Company, 115, 165
n 12
executive branch (U.S. government):
in business conflict model, 5, 10-13,
138, 139; and national security in
general, 6, 13-14; overview of business influence on, 6, 11, 12, 65,
138, 139; overview of role of, 134;
and policy on leftist movements in
general, 15; in statist models, 134.
See also headings beginning with Department of; *names of specific
presidents*
Executive Committee on Economic
Foreign Policy (ECEFP), 33-34
EXIM. *See* Export-Import Bank
EXIM Bank Act of 1945, 41, 104
Export-Import Bank (EXIM Bank):
business influence on, 20, 23, 25,
41, 43-44, 45, 46, 52, 136; Capehart
Commission review of, 42-44, 45;
and export promotion, 98, 101, 104,
106, 107, 135; government support

for in 1940s-50s, 26, 27, 29, 30, 31,
46, 48, 52, 153 n 51; and Inter-
American Development Bank (IDB),
74, 75; and nationalist business influence, 44-45, 53; origins and functions of, 40-42; and shift to "trade
and aid" policy, 67; and "trade not
aid" policy, 20, 23, 25, 26, 27, 29,
30, 31, 40-46, 53, 55, 153 n 51
export-led industrialization (ELI), 22,
23, 46, 64, 65, 71, 139
export promotion: agribusiness in, 92,
93, 97-98, 101-2, 103, 105, 107, 138;
banking in, 92-93, 98-101, 102, 104;
in business conflict model, 138;
Central American governments in,
94-95, 96, 121-22; and the decline of
the Central American Common
Market (CACM), 89, 90-96; in El
Salvador, 93, 95, 96, 97, 99, 102,
103, 106, 124; in Guatemala, 93, 96,
97, 102; in Honduras, 93, 96, 97,
98, 102, 103, 104; and internationalist businesses, 92-94, 96-102, 103-7,
138; and military aid, 97; overview
of support for, 89, 90, 135; and policy on Sandinistas/contras, 121-24,
144; subcontracting in, 92, 96-97,
121-24, 166 n 38; U.S. government
in, 91, 93-94, 97, 98, 100, 101-9,
135, 138. *See also* Caribbean Basin
Initiative
Exxon, 113, 114-15

Federal Operations Administration, 49
federal reserve system, 75
Feinberg, Richard, 41, 42, 99-100
Ferguson, Thomas, 2, 82
Ferrer, Esteban A., 165 n 8
Financial Times, 112
Firestone, 92
First National City Bank, 64, 86, 93
Florida International Bankers Associa-
tion, 166 n 8
Foreign Assistance Act of 1961, 84, 85
Foreign Economic Administration, 33
Fortune magazine, 37
free trade policies, 42, 64, 77
Frieden, Jeffrey, 2
fundamentalist businesses, 82, 159 n
57